AN ENCOURAGING DEVOTION FOR YOUR DAY:

Devotional Thoughts to Give
You Encouragement from Your
Best Friend and Mine, Jesus

Kenton Wendorf

Copyright © 2023 Kenton Wendorf

All rights reserved.

"ESV," the "English Standard Version," the "Global Study Bible," and the ESV logo are registered trademarks of Crossway, registered in the United States of America. Use of any of these trademarks requires the prior permission of Crossway.

All Scripture marked with the designation "GW" is taken from GOD'S WORD®. © 1995, 2003, 2013, 2014, 2019, 2020 by God's Word to the Nations Mission Society. Used by permission.

Scripture quotations from The Authorized (King James) Version. Rights in the Authorized Version in the United Kingdom are vested in the Crown. Reproduced by permission of the Crown's patentee, Cambridge University Press.

Scripture quotations marked (NIV) are taken from the Holy Bible, New International Version®, NIV®. Copyright © 1973, 1978, 1984, 2011 by Biblica, Inc.™ Used by permission of Zondervan. All rights reserved worldwide. www.zondervan.com The "NIV" and "New International Version" are trademarks registered in the United States Patent and Trademark Office by Biblica, Inc.™

This is dedicated to my wife, Jan, who is always an inspiration to me; the members of St. Paul, Grafton for their encouragement, with a special thank you to Dawn Sinur whose efforts made this publication a reality.

EVEN IF THE HEALING NEVER COMES
John 5:1-9 (10-17)

"Even if the Healing Never Comes" is a title of a song. The song has a profound message as we think of health and healing. I would invite you to read in *John 5* where you can observe a man at the pool of Bethesda. The pool had healing properties. An angel was believed to stir the waters of the pool each day and the first person in the pool would be healed. I am sure there were many waiting to jump in! One man, paralyzed for 38 years, was at the pool. We can learn much by observing what happened.

The obstacles to his healing were huge. Everyone was waiting to be healed. What were his chances as a cripple to jump in the water in time? Despite the obstacles, he was there! The cripple came each and every day. He did not give up doing what he could do. He did not lose hope. And because he was there, healing was about to arrive but not from the pool.

Maybe you or a loved one is waiting for healing to come. I have prayed with many a person fighting cancer for healing. I have a voice issue that makes talking very difficult, and at times it is impossible for others to even understand me. Your situation may be much worse. But to me the observation is to keep on trying! Do not give up! The man at the pool did not give up for all those years and neither should we.

Back to the pool, a man walked up and asked the cripple if he wanted to be healed. Then this man told him to get up and walk. What? Just get up? Why not give it a try? He got up and he walked. Sometimes healing and encouragement come from unexpected directions. Many things in life "happen" when we least expect them to happen. Notice, the crippled man did not come looking for this man. He did not know until later that it was Jesus who had healed him.

What a lesson. This miracle was not dependent on what the crippled man did, or how faithful he was, or even on the basis of his pleading. The healing took place solely based on the mercy of God. Sometimes we are told we have to do more…pray more…trust more…hope more…but at the end of the day this story reminds me that it is not us, but HIM. As you and I struggle with situations in life, we struggle not as those who have no hope. For our hope is in Jesus!

My prayer is still for the healing of my voice. This is a daily prayer. I want to jump into the pool! But "even if the healing never comes" my hope is in the Man who comes to us with His love, His forgiveness, His peace, and one day His healing.

GO TO
Psalm 91

Do you have a "go to" person in your life? In my ministry, I was blessed wherever I served with "go to" people who were there to help. How beautiful were the words, "I will take care of it, Pastor!" In the Bible there are many verses that are "go to" verses. I would suggest you "go to" *Psalm 91* this week. The Psalm is just what we need at this time. As you read it, look at the "I will" assurances that God gives us in the closing verses: "I will be with you; I will save you; I will satisfy you; I will show you." After reading *Psalm 91*, Google the song "Eagles' Wings" and listen to the words. *Thank You, Lord, for giving us Your Word as a "go to place" of assurance and hope in our lives. Amen.*

RIGHT IN THEIR OWN EYES

Everyone did what was right in his own eyes.
Judges 21:25

If no one is in charge, how do you know what you should or should not do? If no one is in charge, does that mean you can do whatever you want? In our text that was the case in Israel. Everyone did what was right in their own eyes. The result was chaos and the ultimate downfall of the nation. When my grandchildren were young, they would change the rules of the game we were playing so that they would win. They soon realized that was not as much fun as following the rules! Now, they make sure grandpa does just that! There is a big difference between doing what is "right in our own eyes" and doing what is right in the eyes of God. As followers of Jesus, we are reminded to obey His rules. Our prayer should be: "Help me Lord to see our world with Your eyes." When the nation ignored God's commands, He still loved them and rescued them from their sinful ways. Today Jesus is here for us as well. When we stop making our own rules, and instead listen to Him, He is there to restore us, to forgive us, and to guide us in the right way. May the Lord help us to do what is right in His eyes.

IMPOSSIBLE TASKS

The Lord is with you mighty warrior!
Judges 6:12

Have you ever faced a seemingly impossible task? That is the situation facing Gideon in our text. His people were surrounded by enemies, and they had no leader. That is until God called Gideon to lead. Gideon's first response was something like, "Who me?" Gideon was right in thinking the task was impossible, but the key to success is found with the words, "The Lord is with you." Is there a task that the Lord has called you to do? Are you hesitant? Then you are part of a group that includes Moses, Gideon, the disciples, and others. The assurance that you have as you step out in faith, the Lord will be with you. *Judges 6:34* describes what happens, "Then the Spirit of the Lord came upon Gideon, and he blew the trumpet." This trumpet call was the beginning of an amazing victory. The Holy Spirit will also give you the guidance and help that you need. The impossible becomes possible with the help of the Lord.

NOW IT HAPPENED!

Now it happened that Ruth ended up in the part of the field that belonged to Boaz.
Ruth 2:3

Do you ever have exciting things happen to you? I remember the night I "happened" to go to a basketball game and there "happened" to be at the same game as a second-year teacher by the name of Janice. We have now been married over 40 years. The field Ruth "happened" to go in ended up being the field of her future husband. I am sure as you look back, you can see things that have "happened" in your life. In these extraordinary situations we see the hand of God at work. He guides and directs us according to His will. He often places us just at the right place at the right time and guess what? Something amazing is happening even if we are not aware of what is going on. *Thank You, God, for Your guiding hand in my life. Amen.*

THINKING

Think about these things.
Philippians 4:8

What do you think about? Our thoughts are important for out of our thoughts come godly or ungodly actions; wise or unwise decisions; thoughtful or hurtful comments. As followers of Jesus, we are encouraged to guard our thoughts. Here is a partial list of good thoughts to help us as mentioned in *Philippians 4*: whatever is true, whatever is honorable, whatever is just, and whatever is pure...think about these things. Take time this week to reflect on your thoughts about yourself as well as others. See if your "thinking" is on the right track. The fourth chapter of Philippians can be your guide. *Lord, help me to keep my thoughts focused on that which is pleasing to You. Amen.*

BALD EAGLE

Those who hope in the Lord will renew their strength, they will soar on wings like eagles.
Isaiah 40:31

The bald eagle is a symbol of our nation. As you look at the eagle, it reminds us of what we need as a country. The eagle represents strength, power, and vigilance. As it soars above, we imagine it watching over the nation. We rely on our military to protect us. We count on good leadership to guide our nation, and we are so grateful for our founding fathers. But to put our hope on these things would be a mistake. As our text reminds us, we need to put our hope in the Lord. Leaders may fail us, armies may rise and fall, but our hope resting on the Lord is secure. *Lord, thank You for the majesty of the eagle, thank You for our nation, and may our hope be always founded in You. Amen.*

SUCCESS

There were born to him seven sons
and three daughters.
Job 1:2

How do you measure success? Job had children, great wealth, and he feared God. By all measures he would be considered a successful person. So, by these standards, would you be considered successful? Or can a person with no children and little wealth be considered "successful?" The answer is yes; both to wealth and no wealth, children, or no children. Measuring "success" is confusing. Some consider themselves failures, for example, despite others admiring what they see as their "success." I like the words of *2 Timothy 4:7*, "I have fought the good fight, I have finished the race, I have kept the faith." Our call is to do the best we can do, as we focus on the cross of Jesus. As we keep our faith to the end, our "success" is then secured not in what we have done or not done, but in what Jesus has done for us on the cross.

WALKING IN THE LIGHT
I Want to Walk as a Child of the Light

In the winter, it is more difficult to be outside walking but no matter what time of year it is a conscious decision to be made: "I am going to get my steps in today." On my watch, there is a counter for the number of steps I take each day, so it serves as a good reminder to keep on walking. The hymn reminds us a decision is also made as we decide to "walk" as a child of the Light. The light that is being referred to is the "light of the world" Jesus. Icy conditions can make walking treacherous in winter. The temptations to sin in this world are treacherous as well as we strive to walk in the "Light." As you go "walking" in the days ahead, remember these words of the song: "In Him there is no darkness at all." Then as you step out, keep "walking in the light" as Jesus shines in your heart. *Thank You, Lord, for making me Your child in the waters of my baptism, help me to keep walking in the light. Amen.*

OPEN DOOR POLICY

Return to the Lord Your God, for He
is gracious and merciful.
Joel 2:12

You may have heard the phrase, "Open Door Policy." In other words, anyone is welcome to stop by whenever the door is open during office hours. The message is simple, "I am available to help or talk." How wonderful it is to know that our Lord's door is always open. No office hours! In our text, the message was spoken to God's people who had walked away from and ignored the Lord for years. The message: "No matter what you have done, or how long you have been gone, you can return." The message is the same today for us as well. What an awesome Savior we have! Amazingly, when we do show up, He does not say, "About time." But instead responds with His gracious love and mercy. *Thank You, Jesus, that Your door is always open to us. Amen.*

A BABY!
Let's go see the baby.
Luke 2:15

When you hear the news of the birth of the child, the first thing most people want to do is to see the baby. Each baby is unique in appearance, and especially in the eyes of their loved ones, very special. When the Shepherds went to see the baby, they were excited as well. They heard the news, but then wanted to see for themselves. When you think of Jesus during the Christmas season, what picture comes to mind? It probably is the picture of a child in a manger. Wonderful! Is that the only picture you have? In John's book of Revelation, we have another picture: "One like the son of man, clothed with a long robe…hairs of his head were white like white wool…his eyes were like flames of fire…." *(Revelation 1:13)* Both pictures are important. One reminds us of Jesus' humble birth, and the other of His majesty. Both pictures fill us with wonder and amazement. May we come before Him today with thankfulness and praise and with a desire in our hearts to serve and obey Him. A baby is born, awesome news!

CARING FOR ONE ANOTHER

Am I my brother's keeper?
Genesis 4:9

This text is the response given by Cain after God had asked him: "Where is Abel your brother?" Cain knew what had happened to his brother, and his response only added to his crime of murder. I am reminded of what Luther speaks about in the fifth commandment: "We are to help and befriend our neighbor." Or what Jesus teaches us: "Love your neighbor, as yourself." Caring for one another is a calling that we all have. Many are doing that in amazing ways. Today, let us thank God for those who care for us. Then we need to ask ourselves, who is the person(s) God is calling me to care for this day? *Thank You, Jesus, for Your caring love for me. May I follow Your example by caring for others. Amen.*

BEHOLD

And behold, you will bear a son and
you shall call his name Jesus.
Luke 1:31

When a person "beholds" something, you are only an observer. There is nothing you can or should be doing to make an event come about. For Mary, our text was quite an announcement that the angel gave to her: she would be with child! This would be a miracle of God occurring in her life. The word "behold" captures our attention. In John we hear this word again: "Behold the Lamb of God who takes away the sins of the world." There are instances in our lives in which we are called to watch and wait as we "behold" as God does His work. *Help us, Lord, as Mary did, to wait and trust as we behold Your work in our lives. Amen.*

THAT DAY

And in that day a great trumpet will be blown.
Isaiah 27:13

As a new year begins, I go through my calendar and circle certain days that I want to remember. For example, this week, January 19 was circled. By marking certain days, I am reminded of events in the past and in the present. In our text the day that is being talked about is the day of the Lord's return. No date is associated with it because no one knows when it will be. If you circle days on your calendar, you should circle the day of your baptism. The day of our baptism reminds us that through the water and the word of baptism, we are ready for the day of the Lord's return. When "that day" comes, it will not be circled because it will be a day to end all days.

COMMITMENT

As for me and my house, we will serve the Lord.
Joshua 24:15

There is a lot of controversy over the national anthem lately. I find it rather odd that we should be debating this. The anthem, like the pledge of allegiance, binds us together as a nation, and should be held with honor. The positive side is that it does bring up the discussion of what we as a people stand for as a nation. Joshua is making a statement in our text to the nation as well. He is making a commitment that his house will serve the Lord. Pledges and statements are great, but the challenge is to put this "commitment" into our daily living. Does your house stand with Joshua in this commitment? How would you answer this call from Joshua today? *Help us Lord, to be strong in our commitment to You and Your Word. Where we have failed, please forgive. Help us to move forward as a nation in serving You. Amen.*

ASHAMED

Oh my God, I am ashamed and blush
to lift my eyes to you.
Ezra 9:6

Shame on you! Have you ever heard those words spoken? We may hear those words in the political arena as a politician points their finger at someone. There is an adage that is good to remember, "When you point one finger at someone else there are three fingers pointed back at you." Being "ashamed" is not pleasant, but it is proper. For when we are "ashamed" we are admitting our sinful behavior. In our text the writer is "ashamed" to the point of blushing and being unable even to lift his eyes to God. The words of confession come to mind: "Lord be merciful to me, a poor sinful being." True shame should lead us to confession, as we seek the forgiveness that Jesus alone can give. Jesus then responds to us by declaring our "shame" is gone, you are forgiven in My eyes. Knowing that, we can lift our eyes up to see our Savior's love and forgiveness. *Thank You, Lord, for forgiving me and lifting my shame and helping me to forgive others, as You have forgiven me. Amen.*

BAD DEAL

Be watchful our adversary the devil
prowls around like a roaring lion.
1 Peter 5:8

Black Friday...if you say those words, most people will know what you mean. On Black Friday, everyone looks for a good deal. Who can resist a good deal? Shoppers like to compare the "deals" that they discovered. Sometimes after thinking you got a good deal; you realize it was a "bad deal." The devil tries to entice believers with what appear to be "good deals." For example, if you just cheat a little, you will get ahead. Or, if you steal something, think of the money you will save. These are really "bad deals." Peter reminds us we need to avoid the "bad deals" of sin by standing firm in our faith. Be watchful so that you can say to the temptations of life, "No deal." *Thank You Lord, for being with us! Help us to be watchful so that we say "No" to the bad deal of sin. In Jesus' name, Amen.*

BITTER

They could not drink the water of
Marah because it was bitter.
Exodus 15:23

"That is a bitter pill to take!" This phrase is sometimes used to describe an unpleasant situation. For a child, it might be a yucky tasting medicine, for an adult, it is usually more serious. Recently there were a number of layoffs of seasoned workers in our area. That was a "bitter" pill to take. In our text, the Lord miraculously made the water sweet by ordering Moses to throw a log into it. Life will have its bitter times. In those times we have the assurance of knowing that the Lord is with us. He can take the bitterness of life and make it sweet. On Easter Sunday, Jesus turned the bitterness of death into the sweetness of life. How encouraging to know that the miracle of God's grace can touch even the deepest bitterness of our lives. *Help us, Lord, to be thankful in the bitter and sweet times of life. Amen.*

BLESSING OF OBEDIENCE

If you walk in my statutes...and do them then
I will give you your rains in their seasons.
Leviticus 26:3

Teaching Confirmation is at times a challenge. One year I tried a different approach. I offered a pizza party if they would behave. Surprisingly, it worked! They received a "blessing" for obedience. In our text, the Lord promised the people "blessings for obedience." The same is true for us today, as we follow God's Word, blessings follow. Why? Because God's rules are for our good! Ideally, none of us should need to be bribed to be good, but the truth be told, our sinful nature makes perfect obedience impossible. As a result, we may miss out on some of the earthly blessings God has in store for us. Fortunately, the Lord still blesses us with His forgiveness and love as we turn to Him. Because Jesus was obedient, we are blessed. *Lord, help us to live as obedient children as we thank You for Your blessing of forgiveness. Amen.*

BURNING BUSH

He said, but I will be with you.
Exodus 3:12

Burning bush decisions are ones that once made, there is no turning back. In our text, God is speaking to Moses at a burning bush. Once Moses leaves the mountain and goes to Egypt, things could never be the same. The only question remaining was whether Moses would trust God's direction? All of us have had, or will have, "burning bush" decisions in our lives. As the decision is made, you know that things will never be the same. As you prayerfully seek God's direction in your decisions, the promise that He gives to Moses is yours! "I will be with you!" That is especially assuring to know when you, like Moses, have no clear idea what will happen next. The one certainty is that the Lord will be with you no matter what. *Thank You, Lord, that when we make those "burning bush" decisions You guide us and are with us each step of the way. Amen.*

TRUST

But I trusted in your steadfast love;
My heart shall rejoice in your salvation.
Psalm 13:5

Who do you trust? When we are small, the answer is often our parents or grandparents. But there are tragic cases where that trust fails. We are told to trust the "experts" which sounds nice, but what do you do when the experts disagree? Many Texans trusted their power company, but when the storm came, the power failed. As we look at the cross and the empty tomb, we realize Jesus is someone we can always trust. You know His love is there for you, and the promise of salvation is yours. *Dear Lord, when we are confused and do not know what or who to trust, may we be reminded that we can always trust in You. Amen.*

DIRECTIONS

But we will walk in the name of the
Lord our God forever, and ever.
Micah 4:5

A difficult choice! Two hikers were facing a decision as to which way they would go up the mountain. There were two paths, which was the right one to take? Scriptures speak of choosing the right path as well: "But small is the gate and narrow the road that leads to life, and only a few find it" *(Matthew 4:7)*. How do we choose the right one? On a trail, you will sometimes find white marks on a tree, then you know you are going in the right direction. In your life, make sure the mark of the cross is before you on the paths you follow. No fear of being lost, with Jesus as our guide! Robert Frost wrote this verse in his poem, *The Road Not Taken*:

> I shall be telling this with a sigh.
> Somewhere ages and ages hence:
> Two roads diverged in a wood, and I—
> I took the one less traveled by,
> and that has made all the difference.

TOP FLOOR

But you did not look to him, who did it,
or see him who planned it long ago.
Isaiah 22:11

At High Cliff Park near Sherwood, WI, there is a watchtower. Before Covid, you could climb to the top, or part way up for a great view. I usually like to climb as high as I can, so I can get a view from the "top floor." As you look around your life, what do you see? Maybe you see a good retirement plan, or health plan, or the food in your pantry, or a nice place to live. That is wonderful, but we miss the best view, unless we go to the "top floor." By that I mean we look to the one who planned everything, the Lord! *Lord, may You lift us up to see clearly all that You have done and may we respond with grateful hearts as Your plans unfold. Amen.*

CHANGES EVERYTHING

And for many days Jesus appeared to those who had come up with him from Galilee to Jerusalem, who are now his witnesses to the people.
Acts 13:31

We hear on the news each day how things have changed because of an invisible virus. We live with the reality of those changes. The news of the resurrection of Jesus changes everything in a much more dynamic and powerful way. The resurrection of Jesus was not an invisible event. The resurrected Jesus had many eyewitnesses who saw Him alive. With the virus, we wonder when things will be back to normal. With the resurrection of Jesus, things will never be normal again. Why? Death has been defeated. Because He lives, we will live also. Now that is news to celebrate, and it really does "change everything." *Thank You, Jesus, for Your glorious resurrection! Amen.*

NO FISH

Children, do you have any fish? Try the other side!
John 21:5

If you are walking along the dock and see a fisherman, you probably will not ask: "How is the weather?" No, instead you ask them if they caught any fish. Jesus said these words to the disciples and the answer was no. No fish. He then said to them these words: "Try the other side." How will the disciples respond? How do you and I respond when given some wise counsel? Do we dig in our heels or do we listen? The disciples chose to listen, and soon their nets were full. As you go about your life pray that you will choose to listen to wise counsel. Perhaps the wise advice will be in a pastor's sermon, or in your reading of God's Word or in a friend's thoughtful words. May we all be open to "trying the other side." *Thank You, Lord, for Your wise counsel. Amen.*

Interested in the whole story? Read John 21.

KINDNESS
Clothe yourself with kindness.
Colossians 3:12

Paul speaks of kindness. I used to think of "kindness" in a selfish way. I would be kind to someone, and then expected that person to really appreciate what I did. That type of action is often deceitful in nature. We do something to get something. Paul challenges us to be kind to another person, never expecting a response. One person observed that he could tell if a couple was married by seeing if the spouse opened the car door! Engaged couples were so kind. Married couples seemed to say, "Just get in." Take the kindness challenge this week. Think of intentional ways you can show acts of kindness to someone close to you. How about a stranger, too? As you rise in the morning clothe yourself with "kindness" as you thank Jesus for His undeserved kindness and love toward you.

INSTANT REPLAY

Come and see what God has done;
He is awesome in His deeds.
Psalm 66:5

My physician tells the story of sitting through a baseball game with nothing much happening. He turns his head to look around and misses seeing an inside the park home run. "I cannot believe I missed it," he said. Fortunately, there is "instant replay, "and you can see the play again. Are you missing what God has done? As you look around, you can see "instant replays" of His awesome deeds. Start with the sun in the morning and the moon at night, the whiteness of snow, the sound of a newborn's cry, and that is only the beginning. Look again and see the cross where Jesus died for you. See the tomb, empty on Easter morning as He rose from the dead. "Instant replay" is fun to watch. As we replay and remember God's awesome deeds for us, we rejoice in thanking Him for all He has done and is doing for us.

COME OUT

Saying to the prisoners, "Come out,"
to those who are in darkness, "Appear."
Isaiah 49:9

Playing hide and seek is great fun with children. The goal is to hide, so no one can find you. If you are successful, the seeker will finally shout: "Come out, come out, wherever you are!" The Lord calls to us as well. When we sin, our first response may be to hide. Remember Adam and Eve? We do not want to face the Lord and others. The Lord calls to those who are prisoners in their sin to come. Stop hiding and confess your sin. Then you will not receive judgment, but rather forgiveness. Remember, Jesus died to set prisoners free. *Thank You, Jesus, for forgiving our sin, help us to come out of hiding to serve You and others. Amen.*

RECIPE FOR JOY

Count it all joy when you meet trials of various kinds.
James 1:2

During this time, I have been looking at and trying different recipes. Some have turned out very well and have become our favorites. I have also discovered the right ingredients make all the difference (do not substitute salt for sugar, for example). We all like a good recipe, but when James calls for the ingredients for joy are trials; we have to wonder? How does mixing trials into our lives result in joy? The end result of making a recipe is a delicious dish, but you have to wait until it is done. With trials, we also have to wait until they are over. Then we can discover that this time of trial, which is a test of our faith, results in joy. Our example is Jesus who went through the trials of suffering and death, and the result was His glorious resurrection which now fills us with joyous hope. *Lord, help us in the midst of our trials to see the joy of knowing Your presence. Amen.*

TRIALS

Count it all joy, when you meet trials of various kinds.
James 1:2

Relentlessly, reports are on the news of the trials we are going through as a nation. Nowhere will you hear a reporter say: "Isn't this great!" Joy and trial do not seem complimentary. Yet, in James this is stated clearly to us. The joy is found in not looking at the trial but looking ahead at the outcome. I remember taking final exams in school. They were a "trial" of what I learned in the class. But as I looked ahead, I knew that once the trial was over, I would pass the course. As we go through the trials of today, we may not always get an "A" in how we handle things, but our call is to remain faithful to our Lord, to our family, and to our friends. Knowing that the final outcome will be good, not because of what we do (even though that is important), but because of what Jesus has already done for us. *Dear Lord, thanks for the trials of life that enable us to know again of Your love and faithfulness. Amen.*

CRACKS

You made the land quake You split it wide open.
Heal the cracks in it Because it is falling apart.
Psalm 60:2

For years my wife, Jan, had terrible cracks in her fingers. They were deep and very painful. She tried everything including Superglue. We considered moving to a different climate as things got more severe. Then one day, an attendant in a restaurant noticed her wounds and suggested another product. It worked and the cracks were healed! Many and deep are the cracks in our land: economic, health, divisions of ideas, to name a few. As we pray, we ask the Lord to "heal the cracks." Even God's people know of hardship, but our trust is in the Lord who is our God who is with us even when things are "falling apart."
Thank You, Jesus, for Your healing touch in our lives. Amen.

FITTING IN

Do not be conformed to this world.
Romans 12:2

Most of us prefer to fit in rather than to stand out. To stand out means others will notice you and maybe make fun of you. When you "fit in" then you are one of the groups. Perhaps that is why I like the cartoon, Garfield. In this cartoon his owner wears crazy clothes and acts in strange ways. He is definitely not one who is "fitting in." Are you someone who likes to fit in or stand out? St. Paul tells us in our text that when it comes to the things of the world we should not try to "fit in." We should not compromise our beliefs and the commands of God. To take a loving, firm stand for what you believe, will make you stand out at times. But that is OK! *Help us, Lord, to be willing not to fit into the things of this world, but to follow Your leading in all that we do. Amen.*

PLACE OF REFUGE

Do not go outside the city of refuge you fled to.
Numbers 35:26

Reading the above verse, I thought of our current dilemma of being called to be "safe at home" in our place of refuge. In Numbers, a person went to the place of refuge to flee from the consequences of their sin of murder. How long would you have to stay there? Until the high priest died, and no one knew when that would occur. As we are in our places of refuge, we know The High Priest (Jesus) has already died for our sins, but we stay in our place of refuge to protect ourselves and others from an invisible enemy. We do not know how long that will be, but we rejoice in knowing our "place of refuge" is found not in an earthly city but in the Lord. As it is stated so beautifully in *Nahum 1:7*, "The Lord is good, a refuge in times of trouble." *Dear Jesus, as we stay in our place of refuge, we rejoice that You are our refuge now and always. Amen.*

NOT FAIR

Do you begrudge my generosity?
Matthew 20:15

Since we were little children, we have all struggled at times with a "not fair" attitude. A child will say: "It's not fair that you got the bigger piece again!" Adults might say to themselves: "It is not fair that you got the reward, and I didn't. Why are you so special?" In our text, a laborer complained that a co-worker got the same money for fewer hours of work. Many times, something may appear "not fair" from our perspective. Our text tells us not to focus on fairness but to focus on the blessings we and others received. Rejoicing with others as they are blessed, helps our spirits as well. When thinking something is not fair remember, "Was it fair for Jesus to have to die for my sins?" The blessing of forgiveness and salvation is there in equal portions for all of us. *Thank You, Lord, for Your generous outpouring of blessings in my life. Amen.*

I WILL

Even to your old age and gray hairs
I am he, I am he who will sustain you.
I have made you and I will carry you;
I will sustain you and I will rescue you.
Isaiah 46:4

Are you ready for some good news? I know that I am. As we look at the world around us, no surprise, there are a lot of disastrous situations. The children of Israel also needed some good news with the trials they were facing and many of those trials were a result of their own actions. In the midst of their heartaches, Isaiah proclaims these words of our text to them. The Lord gives you these same words of encouragement. No matter how overwhelming your trials, as a child of God who is a follower of Jesus, you can be assured that "I will" be there for you today. *Thank You, Lord, for fulfilling Your promises in the past, and as Your children today, we rejoice in knowing Your promises are here for us as well. Amen.*

DETAILS

Exactly as I show you.
Exodus 25:9

How careful are you with the details of your life? In many cases, we can be concerned with the big things in life and forget how critical the little things are. If you have ever made something, you know that every detail counts. That is every stitch, every nail is important. Our God is a God of "details." In our text, He laid out exactly how the nation of Israel was to build the tabernacle. God knows all the "details" of your life. As you examine your life, what are the sinful areas that you are ignoring? Knowing that every "detail" is important, confess your sin, and ask for forgiveness and be determined that with the help of God you will change. *Thank You, Lord, for forgiving me and helping me to make every detail of my life pleasing in Your sight. Amen.*

FAITHLESS

In the time of his distress, he became
yet more faithless to the Lord.
2 Chronicles 28:22

One sin leads to another, then another, and then another. Too often we hear of the life of someone who makes a mistake, but instead of recognizing the mistake, a series of cover ups begin. What a mess! In our text, Ahaz does just that. He began to worship one false god who did not help, so he turned to another and then another. How sad! The good news is that despite our "faithlessness" our Lord is faithful. That simple truth is amazing. No matter how far we have gone astray into sin, Jesus is still there for us. Ahaz never repented, but his son turned out much better. If you are facing a time of distress because of your sin, turn to the Lord. As you repent you will hear the wonderful news of forgiveness, and then know the peace that Jesus brings. *Help us, Lord, to be faithful and not faithless in what we do. Amen.*

OUR FATHER WHO ART IN HEAVEN

A Father's Love
For the Lord will not forsake His people.
1 Samuel 12:22

Some years ago, my dad looked into the mirror and said: "Kent, I look like one of those old people." I laughed at the time, but now I know what he meant! Life changes for all of us. We all grow old, and things we own wear out over time. On this Father's Day weekend, we remember one thing that never grows old: our Heavenly Father's love for us. Let us give thanks this day for earthly fathers and together, let us thank God for our heavenly Father. His love is there for us! For the promise is here in our text that the Lord will not forsake His people. Knowing that Your heavenly Father loves you is a love that never grows old and is a love that will never change. *Thank You, Father, for loving us, and helping us to reflect that love in all that we do. Amen.*

TIME

For everything there is a season,
and a time for every matter under heaven.
Ecclesiastes. 3:1

A New Year's Eve tradition has many people watching the countdown to New Year's Day. The numbers going down from 60 to 0 show the passing of time. *Ecclesiastes 3* is a great chapter of Scripture to read on New Year's Eve. In this chapter, Solomon has some fantastic insights into time. The bottom line is time never stops, and each of us has the same amount of time each year to use. How do you use your time? There are choices that God gives us every day in how we use our time. The beautiful words of *1 Corinthians 10:31* come to mind: "whatever you do, do all to the glory of God." Our prayer can be: *Lord, help me to use the time You give me wisely, and may I use the gift of time that You give me to Your glory. Amen.*

*Thank you for taking "time" to read these devotions.
I appreciate your emails! Happy New Year!
-Pastor Wendorf*

CAPTIVE!

For I have learned to be content regardless
of my circumstances.
Philippians 4:11

For two years Paul was held captive in Rome. He was awaiting his trial before Caesar. There was nothing he could do to speed things up, he just had to wait. Today in our world we are waiting, wondering, hoping, and praying that a Covid cure might be found. How long before the cure? During this time, we have the opportunity to better understand Paul's statement: "I have learned to be content." Learning contentment is not easy. As Paul was waiting, he was busy writing and witnessing to those around him. Contentment does not mean being idle! *Thank You, Lord, for our daily provision, help us to use this time of waiting wisely as Paul did. Amen.*

NEVER CHANGING GOD
For I the Lord do not change.
Malachi 3:6

A child will often try to get their parent (or grandparent) to change their minds. If they ask often enough, they are hoping to wear someone down to say yes: "Please, can we go to get some ice cream? Please!" Do you try to get God to change His mind? Now, we do not want Him to change His mind about forgiving us. But do we want Him to make exceptions to one of His Commandments? With God there is no pleading necessary. He will not change His mind about His Commandments or laws, and He will not change His mind about His forgiveness and love. As children of God, we can find great comfort in knowing that we have a never changing God. *Thank You, Lord, that in a changing and confusing world, You never change. Amen.*

FIRST THINGS FIRST

For none of us lives to himself, and none of us dies to himself. For if we live, we live to the Lord.
Romans 14:7-8

Have you ever tried opening a door the wrong way? Approaching a door, you may pull and pull trying to get it open. Then you take a step back and see the sign: "Please Push." Life at times seems very complicated. It does not have to be that way if we remember to put "first things first." Our text serves as a great reminder to us by saying that if we live (which obviously you are otherwise you would not be reading this), we live to the Lord. We often pull and pull at decisions, wondering what to do. Our focus is on ourselves. It is only when we look up and see the sign of the cross that we remember what we are to do. As we put the Lord first, He opens the doors of life for us. So, remember to put, "first things first!" *Forgive me Lord, for so often I focus on myself. Help me to live the new life in Christ by focusing first on You! Amen.*

SUPPORT

For the eyes of the Lord run to and fro
throughout the whole earth to give strong
support to those whose heart is
blameless before Him.
2 Chronicles 16:9

Recently, I was at a beach in Texas enjoying the surf and sun. A three-wheeler came to our location, on board was a lifeguard. He talked with my grandson who was thrilled. What a comfort to know that "support" was available if we needed it. In our text, the Lord is going throughout the earth to provide "support." The lifeguard's support was available to anyone on the beach. How wonderful to know the Lord's support is here for us as well. Though we have sinned and turned from God, by His grace our hearts have been cleansed. Even when we struggle because of sin, the Lord is already there for us. He is looking to provide "support." *Lord, thank You for Your strong support in our lives. Amen.*

THE HEART OF THANKSGIVING

For the Lord is good; His steadfast love endures forever, And his faithfulness to all generations.
Psalm 100:5-6

Thanksgiving week 2020 is here. However, this year the celebration will be different because most will not be traveling to see one another. The good news for us is that Thanksgiving does not depend on family, or turkey, or even pumpkin pie. The heart of Thanksgiving is found in the Lord, for He is good. And He is good all the time! Whether we are feasting, or in a hospital bed, or with family members, or alone, or mourning the loss of a loved one, we have a reason to give thanks. The Lord's love, forgiveness, and salvation are here for us. *Thank You, Lord, for Your blessing of love for us today as it has been throughout all generations. Amen.*

CYBER DAY

For they saw His star in the east.
Matthew 2:2

Stupendous Cyber Deals Today Only! NASA to Land on Mars Today! These star-studded events awaited us on Cyber Monday. Amazing events but they pale in comparison to the greatest Cyber Day of all when the star appeared in the east. A star that would begin a journey of the Wise Men not for one day but for many days as this star would lead them to the manger. The journey was difficult, but the focus was there and even when they faced hostile government leaders, they did not waver. Today, let us do the same. Keeping our focus on the manger where the earthly journey of Jesus began. He is the one who would bring the greatest gifts of all including: forgiveness, life, and salvation. *Help us, Lord, to focus once again not on the things around us but on You! Amen.*

SPOILER ALERT

From the beginning I revealed the end.
Isaiah 46:10

Once I was at a meeting and the leader shouted: "spoiler alert!" What he was about to say was giving away the ending of a movie. If you did not want to know the results, you need to plug your ears. There are times we wished we knew the ending: when will Covid be over, when will I get better, or will I ever get married? In our text we see a wonderful "spoiler alert." The end is revealed by God. In *Isaiah 46:13* we read: "I will provide salvation for Zion." The message is for us as well: salvation and eternal life is ours through faith in Jesus! No matter how tough or how easy life has become for you, we have confidence in knowing the final outcome. Spoiler alert: Heaven and Salvation is ours! *Thank You, Lord, that we can know with confidence the outcome of our lives because of Jesus, salvation is ours. Amen.*

LISTEN

Give ear to my prayer; Listen to my plea for grace.
Psalm 86:6

"What did you say?" How often have you spoken those words? Many a parent has said these words, "You are not listening to me!" As David turns to the Lord in this Psalm, we hear him pleading to God to listen. In *verse 1*, he asks God to "incline your ear." The assurance of God to us is not to fear because He does hear us. He is not hard of hearing, and neither does He ignore our pleas. He responds with His love, mercy, and forgiveness. *Thank You, Lord, for the assurance that You give that You do listen to my pleas. Amen.*

LOOK-A-LIKES

God created man in His own image
Male and female He created them.
Genesis 1:27

Who do you look like? When a child is born you hear comments such as, "She has her father's eyes." When the dad hears that there is a smile on his face! As I grew older, my mother often said I looked like her uncle. Fortunately, her uncle was a great guy! Our text reminds us that no matter the color of our skin, the slant of our eyes, or the texture of our hair, our Heavenly Father looks at us and smiles. Why? You look like Him, are made by Him, are redeemed by Jesus, and you are very special in His eyes. No matter how you feel, or what others may say, that truth still remains. God likes what He sees in you!

ESSENTIAL WORKERS

God has made us what we are. He has created us in Christ to live lives filled with good works that he has prepared for us to do.
Ephesians 2:10 GW

Are you an essential worker? Today we hear of front-line responders as well essential workers in our economy. We are grateful for them, but what about you? Did you know that you are an essential worker? Often, we think of what others are doing, and forget what we have been created and called to do. Through our baptism, we are part of the body of Christ, and each of us has an "essential" role to fulfill. One work I am doing is delivering food from a food bank, others are boxing and bagging the food, and even others are reaching out to those in need for home delivery. Everyone is doing their part! May each of us roll up our sleeves and get to work this day. *Thank You, Lord, for calling me to be an essential worker in Your church. Amen.*

WHAT DOES GOD LOVE?

God loves a cheerful giver.
2 Corinthians 9:6

This passage is fascinating for it describes what God loves! We often wonder what we can buy for someone as a gift. Why? We desire to show our love in some tangible way. Jesus set the example of a giving love by what He gave. He even gave His own life. Why? Because He loves us! We know we cannot repay Jesus for His love, but He has told us what He does love. May we reflect "cheerful giving" in response to God's generous love to us. *Thank You, Lord, for Your gifts to us, may we in turn be cheerful in our giving. Amen.*

KEEP ON GOING

God rested on the seventh day.
Genesis 2:2

Many workers face a crisis of time. A tearful adult told how he grew up with a single parent working two, sometimes three jobs to get enough income for the family. Or ask a young parent caring for a small child, how much rest they get! Very often the call is not to rest, but to "keep on going." In the midst of the calls to "keep on going" our God gives us the example of rest. Where do we turn when we are weary and tired and in need of rest. This verse comes to mind: "Come to me, all who labor and are heavy laden, and I will give you rest" *Matthew 11:28*. Our rest is found in Jesus who knows who we are and what we are facing. In Him, as we worship and receive His love and forgiveness, we can find the peace and rest that we long for. *Thank you, Lord, that we can find the rest we need in knowing that Your arms surround us. Amen.*

LIES

God who never lies!
1 Timothy 1

Have you ever told a lie? One person remarked, "I do not lie." Immediately a wise person commented, "You just did!" We often wonder what is the truth. Fortunately, we have a rock-solid God who never lies. God has told us that we have the sure hope of eternal life. This is not a new promise of God, but one that was made "before the ages began." The sure Word of God is that those who believe in Jesus will not perish but have eternal life. Eternal life is the climax of our faith for we can know that we will dwell in the house of the Lord forever. Is there life after death? Yes, you have the Word of our God who never lies.

GOING HOME

Father, I want those you have given
me to be with me where I am.
John 17:24

Where is home for you? When traveling there comes a time when we say, let's go home. But to get home often means a journey is ahead. My wife and I drove to Texas last winter. When it was time to go home there were 1500 miles left to drive! It took some time to get there, but our Neenah home was here when we returned. Jesus, in our text, shows His desire to have us one day at "home" with Him. What a great invitation that is for us. Heaven is the "home" that Jesus has prepared for us. While Jesus was saying these words, others were plotting His crucifixion. His journey to cross had to be taken before He could go home. Right now, you are on your journey home. How long the journey will take, what the journey will be like, you may not know. One thing we do know as a believer is our "Home" in heaven is waiting for us. On All Saints Day we remember those who died in the faith and are now at home in heaven. *Thank You, Jesus, for Your great love! We can look forward to being at "home" one day with You and reuniting with those who have gone before us. Amen.*

SACRIFICE

Greater love has no one than this, that he
lay down his life for his friends.
John 15:13

Memorial Day is a day we remember those who sacrificed or were willing to sacrifice their lives for others. Sacrifice is a mark of a follower of Jesus as we are reminded of the sacrifice that He made for us. And because of His sacrifice, there is hope for those who we remember today, and there is hope for us as well. So, for those who died on the sea, or on the ground or in the air, for the many thousands of believers who have been killed because of their faith, there is hope. Why? Because for those who died in the faith, as their earthly lives ended, their heavenly ones began! The grave is not the final answer, Jesus is. On this day, let's remember those who have "sacrificed" their lives for us, and as we do so we celebrate their victory over death. Thanks be to God who gives us the victory through our Lord Jesus Christ.

BAD NEWS

He is not afraid of bad news;
his heart is firm, trusting the Lord.
Psalm 112:7

We have all experienced a lot of bad news lately. We see the reports of the number of deaths from the virus, we do not get to do what we want to do, and we may wonder what the future will bring. No one likes bad news. Virus or no virus, bad news happens. Our psalm reminds us that when the bad news comes, as believers our hearts can be firm. Firm hearts are a result of those who through faith have their hearts prepared for whatever may happen. We will not always have bad news, and we will not always have good news. But we do have a faith that is resting on the assurance of the Good News of Jesus. *Help us Lord, not to live in fear of bad news but trusting in Your promises we have confidence in knowing You are with us no matter the news. Amen.*

MORE BAD NEWS

He is not afraid of bad news;
his heart is firm, trusting the Lord.
Psalm 112:7

We have all heard those words said to us, "I am afraid I have some bad news." Maybe those words were said during a doctor or dentist visit, or at work, or on a phone call with a loved one. When someone says those words, our breath catches for a moment. We all like to avoid "bad news!" Our text reminds us that as believers, we may not like "bad news" but we do not have to live in fear. No matter what the news is, we can have confidence in knowing that Jesus is with us, no matter what the news. As you look back on the "bad news" times of your life, thank God for helping you through those times. Then, trusting in the Lord, know that you do not have to live in fear of any "bad news" that comes your way. *Help us Lord, not to live in fear of bad news, but trusting in Your promises we can have confidence in knowing You are with us no matter what the day may bring. Amen.*

MORE FIREWORKS

His appearance was like lightning.
Matthew 28:3

Watching the flash of a lightning bolt across the sky is amazing. In the dark of the night, the landscape lights up! Lightning bolts are the fireworks of God. The angel sitting on the empty tomb of Jesus at the resurrection looked just like the brilliance of lightning. That is hard for us to imagine. Two reactions to seeing the angel are recorded: 1. The guards feared him; 2. The women heard the words, "Do not be afraid." Those powerful words of the angel speak to us today, "Do not be afraid." Why? Jesus is risen from the dead! Each Sunday we can say, "I am going to church to hear of the fireworks of God."

TWINKLE, TWINKLE

I am the root and descendent of David,
the bright morning star.
Revelation 22:16

As a child, perhaps you heard this song, "Twinkle, twinkle little star, how I wonder what you are." The cute nursery rhyme reminds me of the "bright morning star" mentioned in our text which is a reference to the Messiah, Jesus. As you have the opportunity to gaze into the starry heavens at night this summer, look for the brightest star in the sky. As you do, remember this text, and rejoice that the star that shines brightest in our world is Jesus. He is the one who brings light, life, and salvation into our lives. May this "star" bring to you the comfort, peace, and hope that you need. *Dear Lord, open our eyes to see Your light shining in our lives and in our world this day. Amen.*

WITH

I am with you always.
Matthew 28:20

The word "with" is only four letters but it packs a wallop. For with this word, we see an amazing message. Jesus gives His disciples and us the assurance that we are not alone. When someone is "with" us that means they are all in. Whatever we are going through, that person is by our side. A parent will say that to a child, or a child to an aging parent, or a sister to a brother, or a friend to a friend. Knowing someone is "with" us is a great assurance. This is the assurance our Jesus gives to you and me today. *Thank You, Lord, that You are with us always and may we rest and play in the assurance that You are here by our side. Amen.*

CONTENTION

I appeal to you to contend for the faith.
Jude 3

Contention? That does not seem like a Christmas devotion! Most devotions focus on "Peace on Earth Good Will Toward Men." But there is contention in our world about the true meaning of Christmas. For example, this year the governor spoke of the "holiday tree" in Madison, Wisconsin. Interesting nomenclature! Meanwhile, at Rockefeller Plaza the "Christmas Tree" was lit, and "Joy to the World" was sung on national television. In our text, Jude, believed to be the half-brother of Jesus, reminds us to not forsake the message of the Gospel that we have been given. There is no other plan of salvation than that of the Cross, and many will deny "our only Lord and Master, Jesus Christ." *(Jude 4)* At this beautiful time of year may we have the courage and love to "contend" for the faith in our daily walk as believers.

SLEEP

I fall asleep in peace, the moment I lie down,
Because you alone, O Lord, enable me to live securely.
Psalm 4:8 GW

How are you doing with your sleep? How beautiful to read the words of David as he deals with enemies who were insulting and attacking him. We also deal with our enemies, some unseen like a virus, and others such as our own sin or foolishness that haunts our minds. The defeat of our enemies is not found in ourselves, or in a miracle cure on the horizon, but is already secured for us by our Lord. By faith we can live securely in the presence of our Savior who watches over us as well as our coming and going both now and forever more. *Thank You, Lord, that we can close our eyes in peace, knowing we are securely in Your care. Amen.*

I HAVE YOUR BACK

Behold, I am with you and will keep
you wherever you go.
Genesis 28:15

Has anyone ever said these words to you, "I have your back!" The words are meant as assurance of help and support in the journey ahead. Jacob hears the words of our text in his dream as he was leaving his home. I am reminded of Lutheran Bible Translator missionaries leaving for Africa. They have confidence in knowing that they are following God's direction, and that God will have their backs as they serve. Whatever your God-given task may be, you can find His promise in those words: "I am with you." With that assurance, you can move forward in confidence, trusting in His presence.

PREDICTABLE

I knew that you are a gracious God and merciful.
Jonah 4:2

How predictable are you? On this Mother's Day weekend, most of us can look at our moms and realize that often they were "predictable." Hopefully in your life, those predictable behaviors of your mom were ones of love, sometimes tough love, toward you. Most children know they are secure in their mother's arms. In our text, Jonah tells us that our Heavenly Father is "predictable." Jonah wanted to see those evil people of Nineveh destroyed. Instead, God chose to be merciful to them as He heard their pleas for forgiveness. God's predictable mercy and grace is good news for us today. No matter what we have done, no matter how often we have sinned, we can turn to Jesus and hear those precious words: "You are forgiven." *Thank You, Lord, for being predictable in Your love for me. Amen.*

DEALING WITH FEAR

I will give thanks to the Lord with my whole heart;
I will recount all of your wonderful deeds.
Psalm 9:1

There are many things that cause us to be fearful. The current threat of the coronavirus, the stock market, health issues, and wondering what the future will bring. How does one deal with fear? *Psalm 9:1* gives us a good way to approach fear. First, be thankful to the Lord with all our heart, and then spend some time recounting all that God has done for us in the past. Knowing how well God has cared for us in the past, we can rest secure in knowing that God will be with us as we face the future. During fearful times may we rise up with thankful praise to our God who delivers us from all our fears!

STANDING GUARD

I will guard my ways, that I may
not sin with my tongue.
Psalm 39:1

We have all said something, and as soon as the words leave our mouth, we wish we could take them back. Words once spoken are gone forever. That is the reason the Psalmist prays to guard his tongue from sin. Listen to the description of that struggle in the next verses: "I was mute and silent; I held my peace to no avail, and my distress grew worse." Keeping silent is not easy! Especially when speaking to someone who is close to us. Jesus was a master of "guarding" His tongue. He knew just what to say at just the right moment, and He knew when it was better to be silent. We need to pray with the Psalmist, *"O Lord, help me to stand guard over my tongue!"*

INVISIBLE HANDS

I will sing joyfully of the works of Your hands.
Psalm 92:4

Have you ever admired someone's craftsmanship? Perhaps a piece of woodworking or a beautiful quilt has caught your eye. We know someone's hands have been at work! As we look around us, we can also see the craftsmanship of creation. Creation is an example of God's hands at work. Those same hands guide us as well. Have you ever been at the right place at the right time to meet someone, or to help someone, or perhaps His invisible hands have guided you around a danger that you never saw? Today may we join with the Psalmist as we rejoice in the works of Your hands. *Thank You, Lord, for Your invisible hands that touch our lives every day. Amen.*

INTRODUCTIONS

In Him was life and the life was the light of men.
John 1:4

When you are introduced to someone for the first time, usually the person will say your name. In the beginning of his Gospel, John introduces Jesus to us. Interestingly, John does not use the name Jesus at this point, but instead describes who Jesus is with the astounding proclamation, "In Him was life..." Jesus is the author, sustainer, and giver of life. When you meet someone, you politely say, "Nice to meet you." And hopefully you will remember their name a few minutes later. Once you meet Jesus, His name is one you will remember. How wonderful to know that no matter what circumstance may be in your life, you can call on His name.

MISSING LIGHTS

In Him was life and the life was the light of men.
John 1:4

Frustration! I checked all the Christmas lights on the string were working. I then put the string carefully on the Christmas tree, plugged the lights in, and half the lights did not work. Has that ever happened to you? As I looked at those "missing lights," I thought of my mom who died this past year. Her light is missing in our lives this Christmas. I am sure you have "missing lights" in your life as well. The lights on our tree this year still burn brightly, as I am reminded that Jesus is the Light who has come into the world. His light shines in our lives and even the darkness of death is overcome by the light of Jesus' resurrection. May the lights of Christmas this year remind you that Jesus is truly the light of your life. The "missing lights" of our loved ones now in heaven are enjoying their days in the presence of Jesus, who is the Light. Merry Christmas!

STUMP

In that day the Root of Jesse will stand as a banner,
for the people; the nations, will rally to him,
And his place of rest will be glorious.
Isaiah 11:10

For those who worship at St. Paul, Grafton, Wisconsin you will observe that one of the symbols in our stained-glass windows is that of a stump with a green branch growing up from it. That is the symbol of this verse and is called the "Root of Jesse." The green branch is a reminder that our Lord is in the rescue business. He rescued the nation of Israel from Egypt, and He will rescue us as well. We may be cut down for a while, but the Lord has redeemed us and promises us victory. The ultimate victory is found in the cross and empty tomb. Under His "banner" we have the victory now and forever more.

CREATED

In the beginning, God created the
heavens and the earth.
Genesis 1:1

Going outside is a wonderful experience during the spring of the year. We see the new beginnings of tulips and crocuses even as the grass is turning from brown to a bright green. The earth is truly amazing. In my Covid time, I watched a number of fascinating videos from drones flying over various breathtaking landscapes around the world. Our God is a phenomenal creator! The God who created the earth, makes an amazing promise. He has also created a new heaven and earth that is waiting for us one day. The resurrection of Jesus is a great reminder that for believers, things will only get more amazing when we see the glory of our heavenly home. In the meantime, enjoy the earth, keep the faith, and thank God for His eternal goodness.

STORMS OF DESTRUCTION

In the shadow of your wings I will take refuge
till the storms of destruction pass by.
Psalm 57:1

As you watch the California wildfires, you see fire storms of destruction. We witness terrifying scenes of people fleeing for their lives, as the fires close in on their homes. Whole cities have faced "destruction." We pray for all those in danger. I am reminded of the image of a small child in the arms of a parent when they are afraid. Their parents' arms give them comfort until the fear is gone. During those terrifying moments in our lives, we are never alone. In the shadow of His wings, we find refuge. The storms of life may still come, but despite the storms we are secure in the arms of the One who faced the destruction of the cross. Jesus' resurrection victory gives us hope, no matter what storms may come our way. *Thank You, Jesus, for being with us during the storms of life; may we find comfort in Your arms. Amen.*

INFLUENTIAL PEOPLE

It is better to depend on the Lord than
to trust influential people.
Psalm 118:8

Trust me! Vote for me! By now you have received a lot of encouragement from various candidates to, "trust in me." Who should you listen to, who should you trust? In the midst of the messages that we hear, the words of this Psalm ring a great note of truth: "Depend on the Lord!" I am grateful for influential people, and the election results will soon be here. But no matter who is elected, our true dependency is on the Lord. We can rejoice in His daily and eternal provision. *Help us to remember Lord, that we can in the midst of trials and confusion, depend on You for our life and salvation. Amen.*

UNDER TRIAL

Blessed is the one who perseveres under trial.
James 1:12

Recently our nation witnessed the Supreme Court nominee who was "under trial." What a difficult time for him and his family. All of us are at various times "under trial." We face difficult circumstances of life. How do we face those times? Our text reminds us that with the help of God we are to persevere. To remain faithful as we place our trust in the Lord to get us through. Then, once we stand the test, we will be blessed as we experience the hand of God. *Thank You, Lord, for being with us when we are under trial. Strengthen our faith so we persevere. Amen.*

GOOD OLD DAYS

Jesus Christ the same yesterday, today, and forever.
Hebrews 13:8

Well, it has happened to me. I now can say, "Remember the good old days!" Like when I would leave in the morning on my bike, and mom never worried about me. With so many things changing around us we may wish for better times either in the past or in the future. However, change is also beautiful. Look at the fall colors as the leaves change from green to vibrant red and gold. Looking at the past, present, and the future our faith enables us to see something that never changes: Jesus! Today we let "the good old days" roll on because we know that no matter what the season of life, Jesus is with us. In Him we find our comfort, our peace, and our hope. His goodness and mercy will follow us all the days of our lives. *(Psalm 23:6)*

TOUCHING

Jesus reached out His hand and touched him.
Mark 1:41

Jesus in our text is touching a person who was a leper! People were horrified that Jesus would touch such a person. Yet, for that man the touch of Jesus changed his life. Today, I salute those who "touch" others with the love of Jesus. At the Lutheran Women's Missionary League Convention, I heard of a man who went to a foreign country to share the love of Jesus with his family. He saw the elderly who were lonely, and in need of help. He went into a home for elderly, and began washing their feet, cutting their toenails, and dressing their foot wounds. Smelly! Dirty! After a while they began to ask why he was doing this, and he had the opportunity to share the message of Jesus. As many feet were healed, souls were also healed as the result of the loving touch of someone who cared. The healing touch of Jesus transforms lives! *Jesus, thank You for touching me with Your love, and help me to touch others with Your love today. Amen.*

ALWAYS PRAY

Jesus told them a parable to the effect that they ought always to pray and not lose heart.
Luke 18:1

Persistent prayer is what you do over and over again, waiting for an answer. I can think of several prayers I have repeated daily for many years. How about you? Is there someone or something you continue to pray for? In our lesson, a widow finally gets an answer to her prayers. Jesus encourages us to "always pray" and "not to lose heart." We pray knowing He hears us and will answer our prayers.

KINDNESS

Clothe yourself with kindness.
Colossians 3:12

When you are kind to someone, do you expect a response? Maybe opening the door for a stranger, you expect them to say, "Thank you." Paul challenges us to be kind to others, never expecting a response. In the divisive world in which we live, Paul's call to kindness is all the more important. Take the kindness challenge this week. Think of intentional ways you can show acts of kindness to someone close to you or to a neighbor or to a stranger. And remember, no response is required for a kind act! As you rise in the morning clothe yourself with "kindness" as you thank Jesus for His undeserved kindness and love toward you.

FIREWORKS

Let the heavens rejoice and let the earth be glad.
Let them say among the nations, "The Lord Reigns!"
1 Chronicles 16:31

Do you like a good fireworks show? Seeing the fireworks light the dark evening sky is awesome. I love to hear all the oohs, the aahs, and comments such as, "Look at that one!" The fireworks go off, because we are rejoicing in our nation, the United States of America. There was a time in my life I actually was on a fireworks team. I still remember one night the person who was lighting off the fireworks came running by me and simply said, "Run!" I did not ask any questions! We do not need any man-made fireworks to proclaim the wonderful words of our Psalm, "The Lord Reigns." As you look up at the starry sky, or see the lightning flashing, or watch a beautiful sunrise, that is a great opportunity to say, "The Lord Reigns." For the Lord is once again blessing us. So, along with your oohs and aahs, why not shout out the words, "The Lord Reigns and let the heavens rejoice." That is really something to celebrate!

LISTENING

Pharaoh's heart was hardened and he
would not listen to them.
Exodus 8:19

Have you ever talked to someone, and no matter how hard you try, they will not listen? They may be involved in a dangerous activity or continue to go down a path toward destruction by their sinful behavior. Maybe this describes you? The comment is often made, "Why won't they listen?" This is what happened to Moses when he talked to Pharaoh. For Pharaoh, his refusal to listen resulted in catastrophe for Egypt. As each of us looks back on our lives, we will find times in which we wish we had listened. The great news is that we can receive forgiveness for those sins. The past can also remind us today to listen more carefully. We begin by listening to God's Word as an unfailing guide. The next time you hear those words, "Are you listening?" Make sure you do. A lot of heart ache can be avoided. *Lord, help me to always listen to Your guidance in my life. Amen.*

I TOLD YOU SO!

*Look and see if there is any sorrow like
my sorrow which was brought upon me.
Lamentations 1:12*

Did anyone ever say those words to you, or have you ever been tempted to say the words, "I told you so" to someone else? When those words are spoken, they are describing an unpleasant situation that transpired in your life. The worst "I told you so" occurs when we talk to ourselves as our text states so well, "If there is any sorrow like my sorrow, which was brought upon me." When the reality of our sin, our mistakes, our foolish speaking cascades on us, we often say to ourselves these very words. Fortunately, Jesus does not say those words. Instead, He says these words, "I love you so." As we go to the cross, we see the depth of our sins, which led Jesus to die so that we might be forgiven for the times we have failed. Now we hear these comforting words from the cross, "Father forgive them."

SPEAK CAREFULLY!

They sent to Jesus some of the Pharisees…
to trap Him in His talk.
Mark 12:13

We have all heard of the investigation into what some are calling a Russian conspiracy. The authorities are trying to determine what was really said to the Russians behind closed doors. With cameras, emails, and other devices everything we say can be heard by others. We need to "speak carefully!" In our text, the authorities were trying to trap Jesus into saying something against the government. Jesus was careful. His response in *Mark 12* was, "render to Caesar what is Caesar's and to God what is God's." All of us have failed at times to "speak carefully." No investigation is needed, guilty as charged. Fortunately, we can ask for and receive forgiveness for our sins. As you begin a new year, is there someone you need to go to and ask for forgiveness because you failed to "speak carefully?" The world loves to catch someone who fails to "speak carefully." A great prayer for all of us to speak each day is this: May these words of my mouth and this meditation of my heart be pleasing in your sight, LORD, my Rock, and my Redeemer. *(Psalm 19:14)*

GOD'S PURPOSE AND DIRECTION

Now the Lord said to Abram,
"Go from your country and your kindred and your father's house to the land that I will show you."
Genesis 12:1

Most of the time, we get up in the morning with a general idea of what we are going to do in the day ahead. If you are a student, your day is pretty well decided by someone else, and the same is true for many jobs. Can we imagine what Abram felt when God told him one day, "Time to move!" The response of Abram was amazing: I am going. *Psalm 16:11* states it well, "You make known to me the path of life." As we enter this new decade, we are reminded that the Lord is here to guide us. He has a purpose and direction for our lives. So, we can enter this new decade with great anticipation. May we with the help of the Holy Spirit follow His call as Abram did.

CHOICES

My desire is to depart and be with
Christ which is far better.
Philippians 1:23

Which would you prefer? Winter or summer? Healthy or sick? Living or dying? Many would pick healthy, summer, living! Paul in our text tells us the best choice for him is to depart (die). Does that sound strange to us? We all want to enjoy life and live it to the full. Life, liberty, the pursuit of happiness is ingrained in us. Paul's remark needs to be seen through the lenses of faith. Once when visiting a believer who was near death, the pastor said, "Soon you will see Jesus." Her face lit up with a big smile. She understood what Paul was saying. On All Saints Day, as we remember those who have departed this life trusting in Jesus, we can rejoice with them even in our sorrow, knowing, "to be with Christ is far better!"

NOT STUPID

O God you know my stupidity.
Psalm 69:5 GW

Has anyone ever called you stupid? We normally think that using this word is inappropriate. For example, we never want to call a child stupid because of a lack of knowledge. Yet, here the Psalmist David, is calling himself "stupid." Why? He realizes his stupid sins, and he acknowledges the fact that God knows them as well. We all need to acknowledge that we all do "stupid" at times and as we do so we are recognizing our sins. How blessed to know that despite our stupidity, God still loves us. Through the cross He forgives us and tells us we are not stupid, but we are forgiven.

ROCKS

O Lord my Rock and my Redeemer.
Psalm 19:14

Rocks are amazing! This past week Jan and I went to look at rocks to use in our landscape project. We visited a "rock" place and were shown bin after bin of rocks that we could choose from. The colors and variety were fantastic. What an awesome creator God we have. One group of rocks is called rock candy. Interesting name for rocks! In Scripture, there are many gems or rocks for us to look at. May these verses from *Psalm 19* serve as words of guidance for us and may they be your "rocks" to enjoy this week.

OUR FATHER WHO ART IN HEAVEN

Father
Let the words of my mouth and the mediation
of my heart be acceptable in your sight O
Lord, my rock and my redeemer.
Psalm 19:14

This weekend we recognize Father's Day. Although not a religious holiday, the day does give us an opportunity to remember our fathers and our heavenly father. What are your memories of your father? Whether we like it or not, our lives reflect theirs. Ever hear the phrase, "You're a chip off the old block?" Our heavenly Father is one that we all share. His fatherly goodness has been given to you because you are His child. So how do we celebrate? We can begin by praying or reading out loud the words of *Psalm 136:1-3*: "Give thanks to the Lord, for he is good. His love endures forever. Give thanks to the God of gods. His love endures forever. Give thanks to the Lord of lords: His love endures forever." What great words of praise to our Heavenly Father. We can also celebrate by thanking our earthly fathers. Nothing we can give is better than that.

PACKAGE DELIVERED

God so loved the world that He gave His only son.
John 3:16

The doorbell rings, and you look out of the door and see that it is a UPS truck. You open the door, and there is the package. What is inside? Do you wait to open it, or is it ripped open right away? If you are like my grandchildren, they want to open the gift immediately if not sooner. At Christmas we remember the greatest "package" ever delivered. A small boy, born in humble circumstances, is that package. The child is none other than Jesus who would be the Savior of the world. When opening a mysterious box, you may wonder what is inside. But if it is a gift, you know it was sent with love. Today, we give thanks for the great gift of God's love. *John 3:16*, "God so loved the world that He gave His only son." "Package delivered" on the day we have called Christmas Day. Merry Christmas!

DON'T GO

See, we are going to Jerusalem. And the Man will be delivered over to the chief priests and they will condemn him to death.
Matthew 20:18

There are places where we are told, "Don't go there." During our pandemic, many felt that way about going to a hospital. The reason for the caution was the danger of infection from the virus. Yet many health care workers did just the opposite, they went to serve those in need. Jesus knew the danger He faced going into Jerusalem. Yet, Jesus went into the city boldly on Palm Sunday, and a few days later died on the cross. He died, so that we might live. Today let us thank Jesus for His boldness and love for us on that Palm Sunday and for all those who boldly serve us, even in dangerous circumstances, in our community.

PEACE

Peace I leave with you; my peace I give to you.
Not as the world gives do I give to you.
John 14:27

Often when the news comes on, I do not want to listen. Over and over again there are accounts of tragedy and death. Often with many unanswered questions, but the reality is the same, death has come. What we know about death is revealed to us in God's Word. We can know that those who die in faith rest in "peace." Their time of earthly life is over, many times way too early from our perspective. We may struggle with their death, but they are at peace. In faith we then place death into His hands as we are assured with the words of Jesus, "I am the resurrection and the life, I live and so shall you." That assurance gives us comfort, even as we long for not the peace that the world gives, but the "peace" Jesus alone can give. *Thank You, Jesus, for the peace that You alone can give. Amen.*

AMAZING SIGHTS

Peter rose and ran to the tomb and looking in he saw the linen cloths by themselves; and he went home marveling at what had happened.
Luke 24:12

During this time of year many are traveling and taking pictures. These pictures capture unique scenes of natural beauty. The flowers, landscape, and animals in creation are beautiful to behold. The best scene shot ever is recorded here in Luke. Peter comes to an empty tomb! At first, maybe it does not sound exciting but then we realize what that means. Jesus is not there but instead He is risen! Now that is an "amazing sight." *Jesus, we rejoice in Your resurrection from the dead. Thanks for the glorious picture of the empty tomb. Your resurrection makes all the difference in our lives. Amen.*

LISTEN TO THE MUSIC

Let me remember my song in the night.
Psalm 77:6

As you hear the songs of Christmas, do you listen to the music in the music of Christmas? What are the words really saying? The music in the music of **Christ**mas should be a message of hope, a message of joy, and a message of wonder as you hear the news of the birth of Jesus. There are many fun jingles that are sung about reindeer or snowman or a white Christmas. These songs are entertaining, but do not bring the message of Hope. A trip to the mall recently allowed me to hear sacred and secular songs all lumped together. I wondered how many of the shoppers were "listening to the music." Music has a powerful role in our lives. Make sure you listen to the music of **Christ**mas. As our text for today tells us, "Remember my song in the night." As you have opportunity, thank our great musicians at St. Paul as they bring the true music of Christmas to us in worship.

SLEEPLESSNESS

He who keeps Israel will neither slumber nor sleep.
Psalm 121:4

We have all had those nights of tossing and turning as we try to sleep. Assuming it is not something we ate; we may be thinking about real or imaginary situations of life. The drug companies have come up with products to help our "sleeplessness." The best medicine for sleeplessness is found right here in our text as we read that God does not sleep! That may not surprise you but think about the implication. God is up all night; He is watching over you and your loved ones. So, if He is watching, we can relax and sleep, knowing all is well under His mighty arms. Or if you still cannot sleep, spend some time in prayer and God's Word. Your "sleeplessness" is an opportunity for trust and fellowship with your God who "neither slumbers nor sleeps." *Thank you, Lord, for Your watchfulness day and night; help me to rest secure in Your presence. Amen.*

FOREVERMORE

The Lord will keep your going out and your coming in from this time forth and forevermore.
Psalm 121:8

Forevermore! When you talk about someone who died, the first question that is often asked is, "How old were they?" I am not sure why we ask that question, but we do. I guess if someone lived long enough, we think it is ok that they died. Not really! That is why I love the scriptures when it uses the word forevermore. There is no time limit on our lives from God's perspective. He has created eternity for us. When Jesus rose from the dead, the power of death was defeated. So, the great promise is there that those who die trusting in Jesus will dwell in the house of the Lord forever. Our lives on this side of heaven can be counted in earthly years, but from heaven's perspective we live "forevermore." Because He lives, we also shall live. *Thank You, Lord, for the gift of faith and the wonderful news of Easter morning. Amen.*

HELP NEEDED

My help comes from the Lord!
Psalm 121:1

When help is needed, who do you turn to? I remember speaking to a worker who had spent three days trying to fix a machine. No luck! Then on Thursday, he began the day with a prayer asking God to help him. Within an hour, it was fixed. He later commented, "I should have prayed sooner." How often do we rely on ourselves instead of admitting our weakness and realizing that our Lord is there to help? The author was looking up to the Lord, the "help needed" would not come from within but from the Lord. We can turn to our Lord in confidence knowing that the help we need is on its way. *Forgive me, Lord, for too often relying on myself rather than You. Help me to trust in You as my helper in time of need. Amen.*

WIOUWASH TRAIL

King Rehoboam did evil things because he was not serious about dedicating himself to serving the Lord.
2 Chronicles 12:14

Recently, Jan and I discovered the Wiouwash trail near us. The trail is on an old railroad bed and goes between New London and Oshkosh. As we walked part of the trail, the scenery was awesome, but the signs were clear: stay on the trail, private property, no trespassing. Another good reason to stay on the trail was simple: the trail led to our parked car and ride home! In this scripture from *2 Chronicles*, we read of a king who was not serious about "dedicating himself" to the Lord. He wandered away from the right trail. The signs on Wiouwash Trail are clear, and the signs in our lives recorded in God's Word, are there as well. Jesus is the Way! If you have wandered off trail, now is the time with the help of God to get back on the trail the Lord has made for us to follow. We can find comfort in knowing where His trail leads. *Lord, help me to remain on the right trail that You have given me to follow. Amen.*

SEARCH

Search me, O God, and know my heart!
Psalm 139:23

When you turn on your computer, what subject do you want to search? Normally, when you search for a topic, hundreds of sites pop up. There is never just one choice. The Psalmist asks God to do a search of his heart. This is the information that he is seeking: "try me and know my thoughts! And see if there be any grievous way in me." That is a bold prayer! If we are serious about praying this prayer, God will show us places in our heart that need to be revealed. The sites we go to on our computer will hopefully give helpful information. The same is true of God, as He reveals our heart, He does so in love. He wants us to know, and then come to Him for the help and forgiveness that He alone can give. This week, ask God to search your heart, and discover what you need to know. *Thank you, Lord, for the help and forgiveness that You give. Search my heart, O God. Amen.*

DETOURS

Search my heart, O God. Amen
Send the man back.
1 Samuel 29:4

Detours happen! Right now, if you are planning to drive Highway 60 West, there is a detour you have to take. We often think of "detours" as an inconvenience. Think again. The man in our text, David, was sent back from a battle. When he returned to his home, he discovered his village had been attacked, but because of the "detour" he was able to rescue his family. Perhaps there is a "detour" in your life right now. Rather than being frustrated, try rejoicing. Knowing the Lord can use "detours" in our lives to His glory and our good. *Lord, help us to be thankful in all things even the "detours" in our lives. Amen.*

BROKEN ORNAMENT

Shepherds returned with great joy!
Luke 2:20

The broken ornament lay on the floor. Despite years of careful packing and unpacking, this year it was in shattered pieces. For years, the ornament from Grandma had hung in her memory. Now it was gone. Brokenness is a part of every Christmas. The shepherds knew great joy that first Christmas night. Then came the Roman oppression, the young child fleeing to Egypt, and the deaths of innocent boys. The brokenness was there as well. What kind of brokenness is part of your Christmas this year? Christmas is a good time to remember that Jesus has come and, "He heals the brokenhearted." *(Psalm 147)* The "broken ornaments" of our lives are healed through Jesus and replaced with a peace and joy that He alone can give. *Dear Lord, may the Christmas message bind up the wounds of our brokenness with the joy and peace that Jesus brings. Amen.*

SHOUTING

Shout for joy to God.
Psalm 66:1

On the sidelines at a home football game, you will often see the coach and players raising their hands toward the crowds. They want the crowd to "shout" so loud that the opponents cannot hear the calls on the field. Question: "Where do you find the loudest crowds?" The answer: "As Christians around the world gather for worship!" We may not hear everyone but together as we sing and praise our God, the "shout" for joy is heard around the world. Our "shouting" helps to drown out the calls of the evil one. When facing a difficult situation or a vexing temptation try raising your hands and shouting: "Jesus has won the victory, hallelujah, Amen!"

STAY AWAKE!

And what I say to you I say to all: Stay awake.
Mark 13:37

One of the leading causes of crashes is the failure of a driver to "stay awake." All drivers have had moments in which our eyes were not as focused as they should be. The words of our text are words that Jesus spoke to His disciples. They had asked when the final judgment would arrive. Jesus' response, no one knows except the Father, so you better be ready at any time so "Stay Awake!" These are great words to remember, but they require action as well. You stay awake driving by getting off the road when you are sleepy and getting some rest. You "stay awake" when by faith you are trusting in Jesus alone for your salvation. You "stay awake" when you are obeying the Lord's commands. The words of a carol come to mind, "God rest you merry gentlemen let nothing you dismay. Remember Christ our Savior was born on Christmas day!" As we stay awake, we can rest in the comfort and joy of God's Grace.

STONE PILLOW

Early in the morning Jacob took the stone
that he had put under his head.
Genesis 28:18

How comfortable is your pillow? One night Jacob was sleeping outside, and he used a stone for a pillow. That does not sound comfortable to me! I would not recommend that you try it. We all like to be comfortable. We like to have things going our way with no financial problems, health problems, relational problems, or work problems. How often do we ask each other, "How are things going?" We are hoping to hear and say the response, "Fine." Things were not fine in Jacob's life. The future was uncertain. Then he had a dream, and the Lord spoke to him saying: "I am with you…" He awoke, and realized the Lord was in this place, and he did not know it. When you find yourself lying on a "stone pillow" of life, remember Jacob's dream. You may be uncomfortable, but you can rest assured that you are not alone. The Lord is with you, and as He told Jacob, "will keep you wherever you go."

FALLING LEAVES

Surely goodness and mercy will follow
me all the days of my life; And I will dwell
in the house of the Lord, forever.
Psalm 23

Sitting in my kitchen I was not watching the falling snow (although that is predicted) but the falling leaves. Then looking at the calendar, I saw October is nearly over. The thought of the Psalmist came to mind: the days of my life. Our days are fleeting. Some are full of joy. My grandson had his best weekend ever because his grandpa got him his favorite pizza! Other days are not as joyful. The days of our lives keep rolling on for however long our life span will be here on earth. The great news we have is that we will dwell forever in God's house one day. We know that the best is yet to come! *Thank You, Lord, for falling leaves that remind us of Your promises to us.*

COME SOON

"Surely I am coming soon," Amen. Come, Lord Jesus!
The grace of the Lord Jesus be with all. Amen.
Revelation 22:20-21

As the year 2020 was coming to a close, many could not wait until the New Year would be here. There was not any noticeable difference between December 31 and January 1. Yet, there is an air of hope and promise in the air as this New Year begins. These last words of Revelation tell us a similar picture; the author cannot wait until...the Lord returns. Interesting! We wish for many things in 2021, but is the return of the Lord on our list? We know the New Year will bring new things, but will it be better or worse than 2020? The one day we as Christians can look forward to is the return of the Lord. Then time will warp into eternity, and all will be new. That is really the day to look forward to as we say, "Come, Lord Jesus." Until that time, may the grace of the Lord Jesus be with you all!

STOP IT

Surely I will never forget any of their deeds.
Amos 8:7

When you are around families with children, you will often hear the phrase, "Stop it!" Usually, the words are ones of frustration from a loving parent. Today in our text, our Lord God is saying to those who are greedy, or lazy, or adulterers, or apathetic about the plight of the poor, or merchants who cheat, "Stop It!" What is the Lord God telling you to STOP today? The nation of Israel faced destruction because of their refusal to stop. We would face the same destruction were it not for the love of our Lord God who sent Jesus, to take the penalty by His crucifixion for our failing to "stop It." As our Lord God speaks to you today through His Word, listen and obey as a child should to a parent, they know loves them and wants the best for them in their life. *Thank you, Lord, for Your forgiveness and love, help us to listen to You when You speak. Amen.*

TESTING

For you, O God, have tested us.
Psalm 66:10

In picking up our grandson from school, I asked, "How did the test go?" Often, he will say that he got them all correct, and then other times the results are not as good as he had hoped. Testing is good for us. For when we are tested, we are able to show what we have learned. And even when we do not get them all right, the "testing" helps us to remember what we need most of all: the help and forgiveness of Jesus. Teachers give tests to help their students grow in their knowledge. In this world, God allows testing to occur in our lives as well. When you are facing your time of "testing" know that the Lord is with you and will help you. You may pass the "testing" with a perfect score, but even if you fail, know that your teacher, Jesus, is there to help.

DECEITFULNESS

That none of you be hardened by
the deceitfulness of sin.
Hebrews 3:13

One of the warnings that seniors receive is to be aware of phone scams. The callers are very clever and convince you that they are calling from the IRS or from your grandchild in prison or some other deceitful trap. Every year millions of dollars are stolen by these scammers. In our text we are warned to be careful to avoid the deceitfulness of sin. So be aware! Fortunately, we have the promise of God that we are not alone when facing "deceitful" sinful scams. Ask the Lord to help you to be aware of sinful scams and with the help of God to resist those temptations. *Forgive me Lord, for the times that I have fallen for sinful scams; help me to listen to You and follow Your direction when temptations come my way. Amen.*

BEST IS YET TO COME

The heart of man cannot imagine what God
has prepared for those who love him.
1 Corinthians 2:9

Oftentimes we look forward to something that will happen in the future. Maybe it is a nice warm vacation in Florida, or retirement, or full recovery from an injury. Having something to look forward to is wonderful. In our text, we see that God has something for us to look forward to as well. For example, who can imagine the beauty of heaven, or fully comprehend the Grace of God for us in Jesus? You have heard the phrase, "too good to be true." Well here the phrase is, "too good even to imagine." How do we respond? We begin by thanking God for all His goodness that we have already received. And then by faith, look forward with eager anticipation knowing that by being connected to Jesus, "the best is yet to come!" *Lord, thank You for all Your blessings and help me to grow each day in my love for You. Amen.*

SOJOURNER

The days of my sojourning are 130 years.
Genesis 47:9

If someone would ask you how old you are, how would you answer? That was the question that Jacob was asked in our text, and his response was insightful. He used the word "sojourning." A sojourner is someone who is staying in a place temporarily. What a great reminder for all of us today. We often think of ourselves as being inhabitants and not sojourners. In reality, we are here only for a while, our final destination is still waiting for us. Jacob understood this, even though he was 130. The next time someone asks you how old you are, why not answer like Jacob? Then share with them that you are looking forward to someday being home. Heaven is our home, where we will by God's grace in Jesus, dwell securely. Once in heaven, we will no longer be "sojourners." The words of the hymn come to mind, "I'm but a stranger here, heaven is my home." We can look forward in faith to the day when we will no longer be "sojourners."

THERE IS NO SUCH THING AS A FREE GIFT

The free gift of God is eternal life.
Romans 6:23

Labor Day weekend is designed to give at least some workers a day of rest from their labors. Work is not evil but is something we do. We need income to buy what we need because there are no "free gifts" in life. This makes the message of our text so amazing. God gives us a "free gift." What is the catch? Many find it too hard to believe, but it is true. This gift has already been purchased for us by Jesus. His gracious work on the cross was completed for us. There is no work for us to do. The gift is yours by faith! *Dear Lord, thank You for doing the hard work of the cross and blessing us with the free gift of eternal life. Amen.*

OVERFLOWING

The Grace of my Lord overflowed for me.
1 Timothy 1:14

Have you ever had something "overflow" on you? I am a two cup of coffee person, but one morning I decided three would be great. So, I added three cups of water to the coffee maker, turned it on, and walked away. The problem? It was a two-cup coffee maker not three. In our text, we are told how God's grace is something that "overflowed" in Paul's life. He did not deserve or expect such grace to be given. The coffee made a mess. God's grace makes a mess out of the guilt of sin. Are you struggling with sin and guilt? Turn to Jesus! He is here to bring His grace to "overflowing" in your life with the faith and love that are in Him. *Thank You, Lord, for Your amazing grace that is given to overflowing in our lives. Amen.*

GAVE

The Lord gave and the Lord has taken away, blessed be the name of the Lord.
Job 1:21

The words of our text have been spoken at many a graveside. They are words that we hear but may have a hard time understanding. The Lord gave, we get that. The Lord is a great giver. But the Lord has taken away? The Lord taking something away does not seem right to us, but that is what Job said. Back to the graveside, I liked what one pastor said, and I used to say these words: "The Lord gave, and He gave, and He gave, and He gave, and He has taken away." Our earthly lives are taken away, but that is not the end of the story. The Lord gives again, and this time the gift will never be taken away. What is that gift? Eternal life. On this Reformation/All Saints Day week we remember the gift of God's Grace given to us through faith in our Savior Jesus Christ. Blessed be the name of the Lord!

OVERJOYED

The Lord has done spectacular things
for us, we are overjoyed.
Psalm 126:3 GW

What brings you joy? Have you ever been "overjoyed?" A year ago, going out to eat brought us joy, but when we are able to go out again without concern, we will be "overjoyed." Seeing my grandchildren always brought me joy, but when we are through the pandemic, I think I will be "overjoyed" to see and hold them again. One day, when our time on earth is over, we will all experience true "overjoy" as we see Jesus face to face. As we remember the spectacular things the Lord has done for us in the past, we can rejoice. Knowing that the Lord is still doing spectacular things for us today, we can be "overjoyed" even in the midst of our trials.

ROCK

The Lord is my rock and my fortress and my deliverer, my God, my rock, in whom I take refuge.
Psalm 18:2

In my backyard, buried in the ground, is a rock. Grass does not grow on top of it, so I decided to dig it out. After digging for a while, my tactic changed and instead it is now buried under dirt. The rock remains! As we begin a New Year, we rejoice in knowing the Lord our "Rock" is there for us. The dirt of life does not change that reality. We do not know what the New Year will bring, but we can know that nothing can move Jesus' love and promises for you. He is the one that we can take refuge in because He is our fortress and deliverer. *Thank You, Lord, that You are the immovable "rock" in our lives. Amen.*

HALLELUJAH!

Then I heard what sounded like a
multitude…shouting, "Hallelujah! For
our Lord God Almighty reigns!"
Revelation 19:6-9

There are many hallelujah moments in our lives. This year of 2020, we can shout hallelujah because we reached the end of the year, or we can shout hallelujah because a vaccine has been developed. Individually, we all have had hallelujah moments. Some are life changing, "the test results are negative!" Or humorous things such as, "I got a birdie on the second golf hole!" Those are the shouts we make at the small victories in life. Our ultimate "Hallelujah" is described in our text. Here we see a scene from heaven and those mighty words proclaimed, "Our Lord God Almighty Reigns." As you start the New Year 2021 try shouting with me the word Hallelujah as we remember the heavenly victory that the Lord has won for us. *Hallelujah!*

MY SONG

The Lord is my strength and my song.
Exodus 15:2

What songs inspire you? Do you have a favorite song? Many are very motivating and may even bring a tear to your eye. Our text reminds us songs can also be a source of strength. Why? The music and words remind us of what God has done and is doing in our life. In the morning a song such as "Holy, Holy, Holy," is a great way to start the day. "Alleluia" can be a song to sing at any time. "Why Should Cross and Trial Grieve Me," is one that recently inspired me. Our Creator God has given you the gift of music that can be a source of strength and hope in your life. If you are having a great day, a tough day, or just an ordinary day my suggestion is to play a tune that captures God's promise of strength and hope for you.

IMPOSSIBLE IS POSSIBLE WITH GOD

The sun stood still, and the moon stopped.
Joshua 10:13

In 1940, the Communists were in control of Latvia. Thousands of people were killed and deported, and the churches were closed. The country was under occupation for the next 50 years! The situation seemed impossible, but then suddenly, with one announcement, the occupation was over. What seemed an impossible situation became possible with God. In our text, as Joshua faced the enemy, God intervened, and the sun stood still. The God who can make the sun stand still is still active in our world today. When faced with overwhelming or unending obstacles, remember the God who can stop the sun, who can free a nation, who sent His Son to die for us, is the same unchanging God. *Thank You, Lord, for making the impossible possible through Your grace and power. Amen.*

COUNSEL

Then King Rehoboam took counsel.
1 Kings 12:6

Who do you turn to for advice? Often people turn to a trusted advisor. King Rehoboam, King Solomon's son, turned to the old men who were his father's counselors, and then turned to his friends for advice. Unfortunately, he chose to listen to his friends who gave him very bad advice. Rehoboam did not turn to the Lord for advice. How foolish. When facing difficult decisions, never hesitate to turn to the one counselor we can all rely on, the Lord. So often turning to the Lord in prayer is the last thing we do if we do it at all. We should begin by asking the question, "Lord, what would You have me do in this situation?" The Lord's "counsel" is always good and always according to His Word. *Thank You, Lord, for being here to listen and to "counsel" me along the way. Amen.*

GOD ANGRY?

Then the earth reeled and rocked;
the foundations also of the mountains trembled and quaked because He was angry.
Psalm 18:7

Anger is a powerful emotion. During the recent unrest, there has been a lot of yelling, fighting, and marching that are expressions of anger. Earthly anger pales in comparison to the anger expressed in the Psalm. When God is angry the earth itself was rocking! The Psalm shows God's anger at those who were enemies of His child, David. He answered David's prayer. God cares about you as He cared about David. We do not think of God responding to our prayers in such a powerful way when His children are suffering but He does. *Thank You, Lord, for answering our prayers! Help us to use our anger as a force to help others in ways that honor You. Amen.*

RUNNING THE RACE

Therefore, since we are surrounded by so great a cloud of witnesses, let us run with endurance the race that is set before us, looking to Jesus the author of our faith.
Hebrews 12:1

Recently, I heard of a 100-mile race. This was not a relay race, but a solo one. What endurance that must take! This week, the Lutheran Women's Missionary League (LWML) is holding their Convention with this Bible verse as their theme. How appropriate this verse is for our lives and the ministry of the LWML. How do we run a long race or how does the LWML raise over 2 million dollars for missions through Mites? The answer is by looking up, not by counting every step run or by counting one by one each dollar raised. As we look up, we can, by faith, see that Jesus is with us no matter what challenges we face. What wonderful assurance that is for us. We have a cloud of witnesses cheering us on each step of the way, as we look to our Jesus for the help and strength we need.

UNBORN

They shall come and proclaim his
righteousness to a people yet unborn.
Psalm 22:30

Recently on Memorial Day, we remembered those who died serving our country. In many cases, their deaths occurred before we were born. Memorial Day reminds us to tell each generation the true cost of freedom. Our most important task is to make sure that those "unborn" also hear the message of the Savior who died for them. One of the ways we do that is by our support of our school and educational ministries at St. Paul. As we finish our school year, we give thanks for all those who for generations have enabled children to hear the message of our Savior who died for them. We also see that our task is the same: "to proclaim His righteousness to a people yet unborn." *Dear Lord, may our gifts be used so that children yet to be born will hear the message of salvation in Jesus. Amen.*

TEACHERS

They taught in Judah. They had the
Book of the Lord's Teachings with them
when they taught the people.
2 Chronicles 17:9

Teachers have a tremendous calling. In our text, the king sent them out with the "Lord's Teachings" to the people. Their role was pivotal in the revival of the country. Each of us can look back and think of teachers that were pivotal in our own lives. Let us give thanks to God for them today, and to think of ways we can encourage our teachers who carry the "Lord's teachings." Times and circumstances may change, but the critical importance of teachers remains the same. *Thank You, Lord, for faithful teachers in our lives, and bless all those who are teaching this day. Amen.*

WAIT

They who wait for the Lord
shall renew their strength.
Isaiah 40:31

Two children are waiting for their ride after school. One child is very relaxed and does not seem too concerned. The other is very anxious wondering, "Will my ride come or not?" As you look at these two children, which one are you more like? As you wait for something that is beyond your control, are you relaxed or anxious? Waiting is the perfect time to focus on the Lord. Both children were picked up from school. When their ride showed up, they said, "Good to see you!" As you wait, do so with the confidence in knowing the Lord will be there to pick you up as well. *Lord, help me when I am waiting, to have the confidence in knowing that You will come, and my strength will be renewed. Amen.*

AVOIDING SOMEONE

Those who see me on the street run away from me.
Psalm 31:11

When you see someone approaching you how do you react? One person wrote how with one-way signs on some grocery aisles he went the wrong way! He witnessed people "avoiding" him. In our Psalm, David was being avoided because of his sin. He was spiritually sick because of sin. Then, in *verse 15*, he speaks so simply to the Lord, "My future is in your hands." Today, we unnaturally avoid others because they may be sick. Thankfully, we know that Jesus does not avoid us because of our sin sickness, but rather He embraces us with His forgiveness and love. *Thank You, Jesus, for loving us even though we are sick, help us to love others in the same way You love us. Amen.*

WHAT A YEAR

Though your sins are like scarlet, they
shall be as white as snow.
Isaiah 1:18

The New Year gives us an opportunity to reflect on the past year. What do you see? Perhaps you see wonderful achievements and victories, and you say, "What a year!" Or you may look back and reflect on missed opportunities to care for someone, or words spoken in haste that ruined a relationship or a sinful behavior that has affected you and your family. And again, you say, "What a year!" As I look out my window, there is a covering of white snow. The ground and the trees look beautiful as the words of our text come to mind. As you turn to the Lord in this New Year, be assured of His love, and His forgiveness. No matter how wonderful or difficult the past has been, we have the hope for the year ahead. When a calendar year is over, may we say again, "What a year!" As we thank our Lord for His love and grace in the wonderful and difficult times of life.

SAD NEWS

Today is a holy day for the Lord.
Don't be sad because the joy you have in the
Lord is your strength.
Nehemiah 8:10

We have all had the experience of hearing some sad news. Usually, this involves the health of someone we love, or it could be an event that occurred that is disheartening. We have had our share of "sad news" in the past few months. In our text, the people heard some "sad news" as they listened to the reading of God's Word. They became fully aware of their sinful behavior and realized how badly they had disobeyed the Lord. In the heartbreak of hearing "sad news," the beautiful words ring so loud and clear, "The joy you have in the Lord is your strength." What a great perspective this gives to us. We can have hope and yes even joy because the "sad news" is not the final answer. Jesus is! *Thank You, Lord, for the joy You give even when surrounded by sad news. Fill us this day with that joy. Amen.*

ATTENDED

Truly God has listened; he has attended
to the voice of my prayer.
Psalm 66:19

Frustrating! That is the best way to react when someone does not respond to your question. Have you ever gotten the silent treatment or had someone not answer you when you have left a message or a text? You wonder whether or not they have heard you. We can rejoice in knowing that God not only listens but "attends" to the voice of our prayers. That means He responds and answers us. That is a great comfort to us all. We do not have to worry whether or not He has gotten the message. *Thank You, Lord, for the assurance that You give us that You hear and answer our prayers. Amen.*

UNDERSTANDING

Though it costs all you have, get understanding.
Proverbs 4:7

Charlie Brown once said, "I do not even understand what I do not understand!" This statement is true as we view others. We may try to understand someone, but we mistakenly try to understand them from our point of view. Far too often we stand there wondering, "Why did they act that way?" Our text tells us that "understanding" is critical. Our Lord alone has perfect understanding for He created each of us uniquely and He knows us completely. How well do you "understand" those around you? Determine that with God's help, that you will strive to understand and to be understood! *Thank You, dear God, for Your loving forgiveness and understanding of us; help us to grow in our understanding of others. Amen.*

LABOR DAY WEEKEND DEVOTION

An Impossible Task

Unless your righteousness surpasses that of the Pharisees, you will certainly not enter the kingdom of heaven.
Matthew 5:20

In order to save money, many organizations have downsized. That may sound good, but what it really means is more work for fewer workers. So, a full-time job becomes a full time plus additional work in the same amount of time. It can become an impossible task. In our text, Jesus gives you an impossible task. The task is to perfectly obey the commandments of God in action and in our hearts as well. How do you respond? When you tell a boss you cannot do it, the boss might say, "I will find someone else who can." When we tell Jesus, "I can't do it," He says, "I know. I gave you that task not to overwhelm you, but to point you to Me." In the world, we are judged by what we do or do not do. In the kingdom of heaven, we are judged by what Jesus has done for us. He has completed our "impossible task" of perfect obedience. He looks at you and says, "Task completed." What a relief. What a blessing! Connect to Jesus in faith; we hear the good news of His forgiveness and grace. An impossible task becomes possible through Him.

WALKING

Blessed is everyone who fears the
Lord, who walks in his ways!
Psalm 128:1

Walking is usually a healthy activity. Now that the snow is gone, many families are outside, and doing some walking. I love to see small children out for a walk. They usually do not walk in a straight line, and if there is a puddle of any kind in the way, you will see them stepping right into the water with a big splash. What fun! To stay spiritually healthy, walking in the way of the Lord is the way to go. For those who are walking on the right way, there will be blessings. The reality is, we have many paths to choose from, and at times the way of disobedience or neglect of God's ways appears the easiest. Many people choose to go "walking" in the wrong direction, and we have all strayed at one time or another. To see a happy child jumping in a puddle is a joy. To see followers of Christ walking in His ways is also a time of rejoicing. So as a fellow walker, stop to reflect in your own life: Am I walking in the way of the Lord?

WALKING WITH THE WISE

Whoever walks with the wise becomes wise,
but the companion of fools will suffer harm.
Proverbs 13:20

What a beautiful spring day to go for a walk. A stroller for one child and the other two could easily walk. We decided to take a new trail. The sign said it was a short distance to the lookout. About 30 minutes later we saw another sign, the lookout point was still a mile away. Apparently, we went the wrong way on the loop trail! Fortunately, the "wise" mom was prepared with juice boxes and snacks to keep the children going. No harm done! The companions that we choose as we walk through life are critical. Our text talks about walking with the "wise." Someone who is wise knows how to handle difficult situations. True wisdom comes from above! Seek to walk with those who are followers of the Lord who are also "wise" in the ways of the world. *Lord, lead us to choose wise companions and forgive me for those times that I have listened to my own or other's foolish directions. Amen.*

IMAGINATION

What no eye has seen, nor ear heard, nor
the heart of man imagined, what God has
prepared for those who love him!
1 Corinthians 2:9

What do you want to be when you grow up? When you ask a child that question, all sorts of answers may be given. How about you? What did you "imagine"? One thing we do not envision is disaster or disappointment. We "imagine" only the best in our lives. When we look at Jesus' death on the cross, we cannot fully understand or "imagine" the depth of His love for us. His gruesome death brought us life and salvation. We may not know exactly what the future will bring. However, when we look at the face of Jesus on the cross, we know He has a plan and purpose for us based on His love and sacrifice. That sacrifice is hard to "imagine" but it is a wonderful fulfillment of His loving plan for you.

DISTRESS

When the king of Israel read the letter,
he tore his clothes in distress.
2 Kings 5:7

Are you feeling distressed? I am thinking of educators and parents who faced the challenges of Covid, what was the right thing to do? The king's letter stated that he was to find a cure for a man by the name of Naaman who had leprosy. So, he became distraught. When Elisha heard of the king's distress he said, "Why did you tear your clothes?" Elisha had a cure in mind, the hand of God. We all become distressed at times, but then we need to remind ourselves that the Lord is with us. He is more than able to do what we cannot do as the king discovered when Naaman was cured. *Thank You, Lord, for being with us during our times of distress, and knowing You are with us, may we have the wisdom to know what we can do and trust to leave the rest in Your hands. Amen.*

COVER UP

When the people build a wall,
The prophets smear it with whitewash.
Ezekiel 12:10

Cover up is nothing new. Since the beginning of time, people have tried to "cover up" what they have done. You and I have done it, and often on the news we hear about some sort of "cover up" being revealed. In our text, prophets tried to whitewash the sins of the people, but the Lord saw what they tried to do and responded in this way: "I will break down the wall that you smeared with whitewash." Cover ups, by their nature, will not stay hidden forever. Instead of "cover up" the Lord calls us to confess our sins to Him and to one another. The fear of a "cover up" being discovered is then removed, and instead there is the opportunity for forgiveness. When the Lord "covers up" our sins with His blood bought forgiveness, they are wiped out and gone forever. *Thank You, Lord, we do not have to cover up, but rather You invite us to confess our sins and receive Your forgiveness. Amen.*

DANCING

You have turned for me my mourning into dancing.
Psalm 30:11-12

Do you like to dance? When we are mourning over the loss of a loved one, dancing is not the first thing on our minds. We want to mourn. Maybe sit in a corner, or pull the covers over our heads, and have a good cry. Those reactions are not bad and are to be expected. Then, in the midst of our mourning, the miracle of God's grace appears. Jesus turns our tears of sorrow, into tears of joy and our mourning into dancing. When my mom died full of faith in her Lord, I realized she was now "dancing" in heaven. Wow! That I would love to see! Many people I know do not care to dance. All I can say is sorry, one day you too may be "dancing" for joy in the presence of our Lord. *Thank You, Jesus, for Your forgiveness and love that enables us to dance for joy in Your presence. Amen.*

GOOD INTENTIONS

You will all fall away.
Mark 14:26

Did you make any New Year resolutions? We are a few days into the New Year and the question is, "Have you kept those resolutions?" At the beginning of each year, the YMCA is packed with many who are determined to get into shape, but quickly the crowd fades away. In our text Jesus tells His disciples the terrible truth that despite their "good intentions" they will all fall away. Having "good intentions" is a great idea. However, the reality of life is that we often fail to keep them. How do we deal with our failures? The answer is in knowing that Jesus still loves us. Jesus is there to pick us up as we come to Him and ask for forgiveness for our failures in life. Then, with the help of God, we once again strive to keep those "good intentions." So, the message is simple: "Do not give up!" The disciples turned to Jesus, and strengthened by His love, continued on. May God bless your "good intentions!"

SURPRISING GIFT

You will bear a son and you shall call his name Jesus.
Luke 1:31

The story is told of a teacher who opened a "surprising" gift. Wrapped in brown paper was a partly empty bottle of perfume. She looked at the eyes of the boy who gave her the gift, and with a big smile said thank you. The angel came to Mary telling her the news. A "surprising gift" was coming to her, she would have a baby. Not any baby, but her child was the promised Messiah. Mary rejoiced at the news! Later the teacher learned this "surprising gift" was the perfume of the boy's mom. He loved the smell because it reminded him of his mom who had died the past year. Later, Mary watched her "surprise" gift sacrificing Himself on the cross. The most "surprising gift" of all time is wrapped in cloths lying in a manger. *Thank You, Lord, for Your gift given to Mary, to the boy, to the teacher, and to us! Amen.*

BUY! BUY! BUY!

Your riches have rotted and your garments are moth-eaten.
James 5:2

By the time you read this devotion, Black Friday will be over for another year. Even if you found no real bargains, there was pressure to buy something. This pressure to buy will continue until Christmas. Reflecting on worldliness, we are reminded in this passage what happens to all our worldly possessions. They will eventually rot and decay. Are you aware of the two things that never decay? The Word of God and our souls! There is no need to buy either of these. The Holy Spirit has given us His Word, and our faith is a gift to us as well. May our lives be focused not on things that rot but rather on that which will never rot and decay. *Thank You, Lord, for the gift of faith and the gift of Your Word; may our hearts be focused on You and not on the things of this world.*
Amen.

WHAT WILL YOU DO NEXT?

Your word is a lamp unto my feet.
Psalm 119:105

At graduation time, the question is asked over and over again, "So, what are you going to do next?" That question continues to be asked throughout our lives. For example, I am often asked, "What are you going to do in retirement?" Here is an answer to those questions, "I am going to follow a star." When you answer in this way, people will look at you and wonder if you are OK! Hopefully, they will ask a further question of you like, "What do you mean?" The answer is simple, "I am going to follow Jesus. Just as the Wise Men followed a star to Jesus, I plan to follow God's Word to guide me in my path." As followers of Jesus, we can know that His ways are the best.

ACTOR OR REACTOR

Abishai said to David, "Today God has turned our enemy over to you. Please let me nail him to the ground with one stab of the spear."
"Don't kill him!" David told Abishai. "No one has ever attacked the Lord's anointed king and remained free of guilt."
1 Samuel 26:8-9

In our text we see an "actor" and a "reactor" in action. The "reactor" saw King Saul and decided it was a great opportunity to destroy the king. The "actor" saw King Saul and despite the opportunity to kill an enemy, knew that killing was not the way of the Lord. Our sinful nature will often cause us to "react" in the wrong way. For such reactions we often need to ask forgiveness from others and the Lord. We are called to "act," that is, to carry out the role we are to live as a follower of Jesus. *Help us, Lord, to live as an "actor" carrying out the role You would have us to live each day. Amen.*

THE ALL-STAR TEAM

For all of you who were baptized in Christ
have clothed yourself with Christ.
Galatians 3:27

The baseball All-Star Game is held every July. The best players in all of Major League Baseball are on the field at the same time. The team members are selected by ballots. Ballots are sent in and on each ballot, there is the name of the player. Those who have the most votes have the honor of being designated an "All-Star." Here is the great news: You are an All-Star! How does that happen? The great news is that you have been chosen by Jesus to be on His All-Star Team! Through baptism, you have been clothed in Christ. In other words, you are wearing an "All-Star Jersey." Welcome to the team! We rejoice as brothers and sisters in Christ that we have been chosen to the team not for a season, but for all of eternity. What a team, and what a Savior! *Thank You, Lord, for choosing us to be on Your team. Amen.*

BE WATCHFUL

Be watchful, stand firm in the faith.
1 Corinthians 16:13

Our nation is remembering the events of September 11, 2001. When the tragedy occurred, and the towers fell, our leadership realized that they needed to be more "watchful." Safety is only possible if one is "watchful." Our text reminds us to be watchful for the spiritual dangers all around us such as false teachings, which distort the truth of God's Word, immoral lifestyles and wrong conduct, lack of spiritual discipline, to name a few. Fortunately, as a nation we have many who are defending us. As believers, we have the promise of the Holy Spirit to guide us and to warn us of the dangers around us as revealed in God's Word. Our call today is to always remain "watchful." *Thank You, Lord, for watching over us throughout our lives; help us to remain vigilant to the spiritual dangers around us. Amen.*

ANCIENT TRADITION
Breaking bread together in their homes.
Act 2:46

Last weekend as we exited the church we were visiting, my wife and I reflected on the nice service, but as we looked around many were talking together after worship. Knowing no one, we were looking for someone to connect with us. Going out the door, a woman by herself walked out with us so we struck up a conversation! We enjoyed the interaction so much. In the early church, the believers often ate together. What a beautiful way to encourage each other. There are many believers who are in need of fellowship. Let us each practice this "ancient tradition" of hospitality to those around us. Who can you touch with the love of Jesus through a friendly conversation and maybe a meal this week?

INSTANT REPLAY

Come and see what God has done;
He is awesome in His deeds.
Psalm 66:5

By watching a sporting event on TV, you have the advantage of having "instant replay." No worries about missing the play of the game. Are you missing what God has done? As you look around, you can see "instant replays" of His awesome deeds. Start with the sun in the morning and the moon at night, the whiteness of snow, the sound of a newborn's cry, and that is only the beginning. Look again and see the cross where Jesus died for you. See the tomb, empty on Easter morning as He rose from the dead. "Instant replay" is fun to watch. As we replay and remember God's awesome deeds for us, we rejoice in thanking Him for all He has done and is doing for us. His grandeur and majesty, kindness, and love, are replayed over and over again.

FAST SERVICE

Make haste to help me, Oh Lord my Salvation.
Psalm 38:22

Recently, we needed repair work on our refrigerator. We found a reputable company and were told the next appointment would be in 10 days! Maybe I should try and fix it myself! When given the choice to wait or have fast service, which do you prefer? The Psalmist, for example, wanted "fast service" from the Lord. The key he knew was not how fast, but what kind of help he would receive. Earlier in *Psalm 38* it is stated in this way, "but I wait with hope for you, O Lord." Despite the desire for "fast service" in answer to his prayer, the Psalmist was willing to wait because he knew the Lord would do the right thing. As we wait, we can know for sure that we have someone we can trust in to answer our call. *Help us, Lord, in our desires for fast service, to trust in You even if it means waiting. Amen.*

TRIALS

Count it all joy, when you meet
trials of various kinds.
James 1:2

Relentlessly, reports are on the news of the trials we are going through as a nation. Nowhere will you hear a reporter say, "Isn't this great!" Joy and trial do not seem complimentary. Yet, in James this is stated clearly to us. The joy is found in not looking at the trial but looking ahead at the outcome. I remember taking final exams in school. They were a "trial" of what I learned in the class, but as I looked ahead, I knew that once the trial was over, I would pass the course. As we go through the trials of today, we may not always get an "A" in how we handle things, but our call is to remain faithful to our Lord, to our family, and to our friends. Knowing that the final outcome will be good, not because of what we do (even though that is important), but because of what Jesus has already done for us. *Dear Lord, thanks for the trials of life that enable us to know again of Your love and faithfulness. Amen.*

ADVICE

Do everything in the name of the Lord Jesus.
Colossians 3:17

What are some good words of advice you have been given? Here is some advice you may have heard: look both ways before crossing the road; do your best; be kind. These words are helpful, but the best advice is given here in our text, "Do everything in the name of Jesus." In all aspects of our lives, Jesus is there with us. When we look at what we are doing or what we are contemplating to do, a good question to ask is whether or not this activity is following this advice. *Help us, Lord, to make wise decisions and to follow the advice that You give us in God's Word. Amen.*

JESUS KNOWS YOU!

I have engraved you on the palms of my hands.
Isaiah 49:16

Did you ever try writing something on your hand so that you do not forget? Once I had surgery on my leg and the nurse put a mark on my leg. I asked, "Why?" The nurse stated so the doctor does not operate on the wrong one! As we begin this Lenten season, let us not lose sight of an incredible fact. Jesus has engraved your name on His hand. Why? Because you are important to Him, and He wants you to know that He knows who you are. Next to His nail pierced hand you can find your name. What an amazing love!

RULES OF THE ROAD

Give me understanding that I may
learn your commandments.
Psalm 119:73

When taking my first drivers test, one of the required readings was called, "The Rules of the Road." Knowing the rules enables you to travel safely. The prayer in our text is for understanding of God's commandments. The author knows that it is crucial to learn what God's rules are. Why? So that he could travel safely through life on the road to heaven. Too often the "rules of the road" are ignored when driving. God's Commandments are good and are there for our protection and guidance. Let us not ignore these rules, but join the Psalmist in praying: *"Lord, give me understanding that I may learn Your commandments."*

GIVING THANKS, ALWAYS!

Giving thanks always and for
everything to God the Father.
Ephesians 5:20

A *Thanksliving* lesson...how easy is it to give thanks always? A child was looking at their plate filled with Thanksgiving food: turkey, peas, dressing, and sweet potatoes. Looks wonderful, right? Except the child was hoping for pizza! The child was asked to pray, and after a pause said, "Thank You, God for this colorful meal." There is indeed always something to be thankful for! At Thanksgiving we give thanks as a nation which is good. Better still is the opportunity, as a follower of Jesus, to have *thanksliving* lives throughout the year. Each day is a gift from God and a reason to give thanks to God the Father in the name of Jesus.

BAD NEWS

He is not afraid of bad news; His heart
is firm, trusting in the Lord.
Psalm 112:7

There has been a lot of bad news lately, such as the number of deaths due to the virus, or the economic uncertainty, or the talk about a second wave of infections. No one likes bad news, but virus or no virus, bad news happens. Our Psalm reminds us that when the bad news comes as believers our hearts can be firm. Firm hearts are a result of those who through faith have their hearts prepared for whatever may happen. We will not always have bad news, and we will not always have good news. But we do have a faith that is trusting in the assurance of the good news of Jesus. *Help us, Lord, not to live in fear of bad news. Trusting in Your promises, give us confidence knowing You are with us no matter the news. Amen.*

WEAKNESS

I will not boast except of my weakness.
2 Corinthians 12:5

When you greet someone after a contest, what do you say? My guess is you ask if they won. You usually do not ask someone if they lost. We laud those who win, but the word loser is usually a negative concept. In our text, this is turned around in a powerful way when Paul says, "I will not boast." As Paul realized his own weakness, he understood how much he needed the Lord. When in my weakness I sin, I realize how much I need Jesus' forgiveness. When I cross the finish line last, how wonderful to know there is the Lord who is still cheering me on. When my weak body faces death, how beautiful to hear the words of Jesus, "Welcome home." Weakness brings us to our knees, and into the arms of Jesus. *Help me, Lord, to appreciate my weakness for it reminds me of my need for Your grace and love. Amen.*

GRIEVOUS TRIALS

In this you rejoice, though now for a little while, if necessary, you have been grieved by various trials.
1 Peter 1:6

You do not have to go very far to see someone suffering a grievous trial. There are news stories daily of those fleeing persecution, hospitals filled to capacity, and loved ones battling illness. What great assurance these words of our text are to a believer! As "grievous trials" try to overwhelm us, we can with the help of God stand firm in our faith. We rejoice in knowing that those trials last for a while, but we can rejoice in knowing our future is secure in Jesus' hands.

FILL UP

May the God of hope fill you with all joy and
peace in believing, so that by the power of
the Holy Spirit may abound in hope.
Romans 15:13

Each of us needs a "fill up" in our lives. With all the news and heartache, at times we can be overwhelmed with grief or worry. In the midst of our struggles, especially when our lives seem to be on empty, we have the promise of the Holy Spirit. The Holy Spirit is one who brings us the joy and peace that we need. How? The Spirit points us to the God of hope. We have a hope that is not anchored in the circumstances of our lives or the world around us but is anchored in our faith. Our hope is found in Christ. Having a tough day? Ask the Holy Spirit to "fill you up" with Hope! *Thank You, Lord, for the fill ups that You give in our lives. Amen.*

MOURNING WITH JOY

I will turn their mourning into gladness;
I will give them comfort and joy instead of sorrow.
Jeremiah 31:13

On Good Friday, those who loved Jesus were in mourning. They could not comprehend that Sunday was coming. Throughout the weeks before the crucifixion, there is a lot of mourning. Jesus, Himself, wept at the tomb of Lazarus. Jesus wept as He walked into Jerusalem. Peter was sorrowful because of his denial of Jesus; and the women on the way to the tomb on Easter morning were full of worry. Today, we look around us, and we can also find some good reasons to be in mourning. The exciting news we have is that we know that Sunday, Easter, is coming. Even in the depth of our mourning, we look up with tears of joy knowing that Jesus Christ is Risen from the dead. Nothing can take that joy away! *Thank You, Jesus, for the comfort and joy that Your resurrection brings. Amen.*

OUTCOME

Obtaining the outcome of your faith,
the salvation of your souls.
1 Peter 1:9

When you make an investment, you are very interested in what type of return you will receive. I have found that there are predictions made, but the final answer is something like this: "of course there are no guarantees." Happily, the outcome of our faith is guaranteed. Your salvation is secure because Jesus gave His own blood for you! Our salvation is both purchased and preserved by God. True faith secures our salvation. That is a guarantee you can count on.

A LESSON IN THANKSLIVING

Oh give thanks to the Lord, for he is good.
Psalm 107

Thankful list. What are you thankful for? Take a moment and make a list for yourself, then ask a family member or friend for what they are thankful. At the top of the list, you will often hear things like family, or friends, or health, or food, or our nation. When we reflect on our list, there is a lot to be thankful for in our lives! Looking at *Psalm 107*, we are reminded of what should be number one on our list. As we live "thanksliving" lives, our number one gift is the best gift of all: Jesus! During this season we call Thanksgiving, we remember our list begins with the Lord who has given us the greatest gifts of all—forgiveness, life, and salvation.

PRAY FOR ME (PART 1)

We have not ceased to pray for you.
Colossians 1:9

Do you have family members or friends that you pray for? Do you know what to pray for? Looking at *Colossians 1*, we hear these words, "asking that you may be filled with the knowledge of his will in all spiritual wisdom and understanding." Reflecting on these words, we see how important this is for us. We, above all, as followers of Jesus, want to know and do His will. To do that, we need to pray for ourselves and others to have this true understanding for our daily living. This is a great daily petition that you can pray for your grandchild, spouse, neighbor, pastor, or friend. Make it an important part of your daily time of prayer.

PRAY FOR ME (PART 2)

We have not ceased to pray for you.
Colossians 1:9

What do you pray for? Who do you pray for? Daily prayer is an important part of our lives, but often we can be lost for words. Continuing the thoughts in *Colossians 1:9* is this important petition: "to walk in a manner worthy of the Lord, fully pleasing to him." What parent would not want this for their child? What follower of Jesus would not want that happening in their lives? As we walk with the Lord, in the light of His word, may we lift our hearts in prayer asking Him to direct our lives and the lives of all those whom we love.

PRAY FOR ME (PART 3)

We have not ceased to pray for you.
Colossians 1:9

When asked to pray for someone in a very difficult situation, what do you pray? This can be especially true with a long-term illness or when a tragedy strikes. God's Word gives us great guidance. Looking at these words for *Colossians 1:11*, "May you be strengthened with all power, according to his glorious might, for all endurance and patience with joy, giving thanks to the Father who has qualified you to share in the inheritance of the saints in light." These words beautifully encapsulate our thoughts for those who are facing trials. Note how they point to the promise of our eternal inheritance one day, when all the challenges and trials of life will be over. What a great petition to keep in mind when you are asked to, "Pray for me."

AMAZING PICTURES

Peter rose and ran to the tomb and looking in he saw the linen cloths by themselves; and he went home marveling at what had happened.
Luke 24:12

After a year of little travel, many are using the summer months as a time to go somewhere. You see many of these travelers with their cell phones out taking pictures. Unique landscapes and wildlife are shared with others and saved for future viewing. The best scene ever shot is recorded here in Luke. Peter comes to an empty tomb! At first, maybe it does not look exciting but then we realize what this means. Jesus is not there but instead He is Risen! Now that is an "amazing picture." *Dear Jesus, we rejoice in Your resurrection from the dead. Thanks for the glorious picture of the empty tomb. Amen.*

GOOD LAND

Praise the Lord your God for the
good land He has given you.
Deuteronomy. 8:10

The headlines of the week are usually not ones of joy, but of sorrow, heartache, conflict, and problems in our nation. Nestled in that news is the desire of so many to enter our nation and become citizens. Those men and women see something we have lost sight of which is mentioned in our text: the good land God has given us. As we near the end of the year, may we all have a spirit of thankfulness for our nation that is a gift from Almighty God. *Lord, thank You for our good land; help us to have a heart of thankfulness for Your blessings. Amen.*

MY RIGHTS

Therefore, if food makes my brother stumble,
I will never eat meat.
1 Corinthians 8:13

Very often in the midst of the various conflicts of today, you hear the statement, "My Rights." An example of that is the rise in violence by some disgruntled passengers on airplanes. One of the controversies of the day in Paul's time is what you should or should not eat. Paul responds to this controversy by changing the focus from "my rights" to what might make my brother stumble. He is even willing to give up meat! As we consider our stance on various issues of our day, do we overlook the needs of our sisters and brothers? Jesus never thought of himself first. May we, with the help of God, not focus on "my rights," but be concerned that my actions do not cause someone to stumble.

TOO LOUD?

O Rejoice, Ye Christians, Loudly
Luke 2:10-14

Do you like noisy places or quiet places? If you go to hear an orchestra, it is usually very quiet in the audience, but if you go to a venue at Summer Fest, the music is loud. Looking at the title of this hymn reminds us that regardless of your preference, there is a time to be boisterous. As we remember all that God has done for us, we have a reason to be loud. Over the din of the Christmas music, we are to shout the reason for the celebration. I am sure the heavenly hosts announcing the birth of Jesus to the shepherds were not quiet! May the world hear our shouts of joy and ask, "Why are those Christians so loud?"

HE IS ALIVE?

We walk by faith and not by sight.
2 Corinthians 5:7

The message began to circulate amongst the disciples and others that Jesus' body was no longer in the tomb. The reports in to the disciples on that Easter morning, included an angel that was seen at the tomb! And then others had even seen Jesus. Jesus then appeared to more of the disciples, and the message changed from a question mark to an exclamation mark. He is alive! Seeing was believing for many of the disciples. Today we rejoice with them, but also by faith know it is true. Jesus rose from the dead, and makes the wonderful promise that because He lives, we shall live also. One day, in heaven, we too will be able to see Jesus with our own eyes. As we remember those who died in the faith before us, we can rejoice because they have the wonderful combination of faith and sight as they see Jesus. They are the blessed ones on this Easter morning!

WATCH WHAT YOU SAY!

Whoever keeps his mouth and his tongue
keeps himself out of trouble.
Proverbs 21:23

The guidance of our text is one that is so true in our lives today. Now, with all the electronic means of preserving forever what we say and do, "watching what you say" is even more important. Last week a game show host was removed for "what he said" some years ago. How often have you and I said something that got us in trouble? In the world, there seems to be no forgiveness available to those who speak errantly. We need to chart a different course. Knowing the forgiveness we receive through Jesus, we are called to forgive ourselves and others when they fail to, "watch what you say." *Thank You, Lord, for the forgiveness You give for those times we speak in sinful ways. Amen.*

UNLIMITED

With the Lord there is mercy
and with him there is unlimited forgiveness.
Psalm 130 GW

When you hear the word unlimited, you might think of the internet. There are companies who advertise "unlimited" internet. Of course, there is a fee for this service. As we deal with our own struggles, we often find that our temper, our patience, and our good attitudes are not unlimited. All of us will at some time fail especially as the pandemic continues. Unfortunately, with "unlimited" internet, sometimes a person's foolish behavior and sin are shown for all to see. Fortunately, there is "unlimited" forgiveness found in Jesus. The amazing event of Jesus' death paid the fee for this forgiveness. We can find hope in this forgiveness for ourselves, and as we extend that forgiveness to others. *Thank You, Lord, for Your unfailing love, mercy, and unlimited forgiveness. Amen.*

TEMPTED

How can I do this great wickedness
and sin against God?
Genesis 39:9

The verse of our text is one to memorize! These are the words that Joseph spoke when he faced temptation. Note he did not say, "no one will notice" or "everyone does it." Instead, he put the focus on his relationship to God. When faced with temptations, how will you respond? Thankfully, the Lord does not abandon us when we are tempted. Ask the Lord to help you to remember these words, "How can I do this great wickedness and sin against God?" How wonderful to know we do not have to face temptation alone and to know the forgiveness that Jesus offers for the times we fail when facing temptation.

ADVERSITY

So when Joseph came to his brothers…
they took him and threw him into a pit.
Genesis 37:23-24

All of us have faced times of adversity. You may remember the time the phone rang, or the doctor came into the room with bad news, or the fire alarm went off. Joseph's adversity began when he went to see his brothers wearing his coat of many colors. Then disaster struck they attacked him and threw him into a pit and sold him as a slave. Despite what he was going through, the Lord was with Joseph. In the midst of the adversities of life we have hope. From the adversity of the cross, Jesus brings the promise of forgiveness, life, and salvation. As you go through whatever adversity that you may face, know that despite what the world throws at you, you worship the One who faced adversity and knows your pain and brings you hope!

GODLY ADVICE

So Moses listened to the voice of his father-in-law
and did all that he had said.
Exodus 18:24

How do you react when someone gives you advice that is unsolicited? If you are like me, sometimes I bristle when someone suggests I am doing something the wrong way. Comically, we hear that when men, looking lost, often say, "I know where I am going, thank you!" Moses, a great leader of millions of people, humbled himself and listened to his father-in-law. Is there someone in your life, who is giving you some godly advice? Are you listening? *Help me, Lord, to listen to the guidance that You give in Your Word, and through others. Amen.*

ENGRAVED

As a jeweler engraves signets, so you shall engrave
two stones with the names of the sons of Israel.
Exodus 28:11

Do you have any items that are engraved? When I bought my wedding ring the ring was engraved with the date of my wedding. That engraving has come in handy! In our text, God instructed that the names of the tribes of Israel be engraved on two stones. The high priest then wore the stones on his shoulders. This scripture foreshadows how Jesus would carry our names on His shoulders. As we look at the cross, we see He remembers us! Your name and mine were on His shoulders as He died so that we might be forgiven and restored. *Thank You, Lord, for remembering us, help us never to forget that love. Amen.*

READY, SET, GO

And God said to Abram, "Go."
Genesis 12:1

Ready, Set, Go. When a race begins, you will often hear these words spoken by the starter. Those who are waiting to run are all lined up ready to go. As we begin our year 2022, these words are also ours. Ready (or not) we begin a journey into the unknown territory of another year. When Abram heard the word of God to *go*, he was ready, and responded by moving his entire household. As we reflect on his actions, can we do the same in our lives? Each day, and each year, as we begin, our calling is the same as Abram's, "Lord, what would you have me do this day?" By doing that, we recognize who is in control, and are asking God for the guidance we need. We may not know the direction we will go, or what the outcome may be, but we can move ahead in faith and trusting in God's direction.

NO

God said, "No, but Sarah your wife
shall bear you a son.
Genesis 17:19

Do you like to hear the word, "No?" If we are wise, we understand that "no" is often a good thing. "No" can keep us from doing things that may be harmful to ourselves or others. In our text, God says no to Abram and his plan. Why? God had a better plan that would bless him beyond his wildest dreams! As you ask the Holy Spirit to guide you, there will be a "no" or two along the way. As that happens, remember that with the Lord, the best plan is already there for us. We can only imagine how those plans will unfold for us, but we know the final destination. Jesus tells us in *John 14:2*, "I go to prepare a place for you, and I will come back to take you to be where I am." Heaven is God's "yes" for us.

CHOICES

If you will not obey the voice of the Lord,
your God…then all these curses shall
come upon you and overtake you.
Deuteronomy 28:15

We all have choices to make in our lives. Should we follow the commands of our Lord, or should we go our own way? In our text in Deuteronomy, the choices are laid out very simply: obey and be blessed or disobey and be cursed. Another way to state it would be: do you want to be healthy and free, or sickly and enslaved? The decision should be a no brainer, but far too often in our lives we make wrong "choices." Despite our choices, our amazing God brings us hope. Jesus has taken the curse of our poor choices on Himself! We do not have to pay the penalty, Jesus already has! Are you making right choices in your life today? Ask God to help you make wise "choices" in all that you do.

STORIES

O God, we have heard with our ears,
our fathers have told us,
what deeds you performed in their days of old.
Psalm 44:1

Do you enjoy sharing stories? Often, we try to outdo others' stories, with something that happened to us. In our text, the stories being told are ones that God had done in their lives. These can become a powerful witness of God's activity in your life as well and encourage others to see the same in their lives. God stories also help to open the door to a discussion of faith. May all of us be anxious to share stories of the ways God touches our life each day. Help me, Lord, to see You're working every day in my life. My grandchildren in Texas love to say with me as the sun rises in the morning, "God did it again!"

GIVING YOUR WORD

You are witnesses against yourselves
that you have chosen to serve Him. And
they said, "We are all witnesses."
Joshua 24:22

There was a time when "giving your word" meant something. Instead of a long legal document, there would be a handshake. Promises were made and kept. In our text, the nation of Israel "gave their word" to Joshua to serve the Lord, but tragically that promise was only kept for a short time. Giving one's word is easy, keeping it is often hard. How have you done in keeping your word to others and to the Lord? Fortunately, there is hope. As you and I recognize our failure to keep our word to God and others, seek the forgiveness that Jesus has promised to give. And as you live each day, ask the Lord to help you keep your promise of faithfulness to Him.

WHAT SEEMS RIGHT TO YOU?

In those days there was no king in Israel.
Everyone did what was right in his own eyes.
Judges 21:25

The closing words of the book of Judges are, "everyone did what was right in his own eyes." Does that sound familiar today? As one looks at the murders, the sexual immorality, or the speaking of evil toward one another, we see our situation is no different. Unfortunately, we have to admit, that often times we can be a part of rather than apart from these sinful actions. The world described in our text is the one Jesus came into. He lived and then died to show His great love for us. There is hope for you, and for this world, because Jesus has overthrown the power of evil. He proclaimed His victory and throws His arms around you! That great love does not seem right, because of what we have done, but that is exactly what Jesus has come to give to you as a child of God. That is the Good News we need to hear today.

FATHER'S DAY

I believe in God the Father Almighty,
Maker of heaven and earth.
The First Article of the Apostles' Creed

This weekend we recognize Sunday as "Father's Day." What a great opportunity to remember our earthly father as well as our heavenly Father. What do you give your earthly father, if he is living, on Father's Day? Good question and one that many merchants are eager to answer! Can you give our heavenly Father a gift? Martin Luther reminds us that the gift our heavenly Father cherishes are words of thanks and praise as well as a desire to serve and follow His commands. What a great gift idea for our earthly fathers as well. That we share words of thanks for all that they have done for us, and that we listen and follow the godly advice that they have given to us. *Thank You, Lord, for our earthly fathers and their love for us; thank You heavenly Father for Your unconditional love toward us and the many blessings that You continually give to us. Amen.*

NO REGRETS

Saul said to Samuel, "I have sinned, for I
have transgressed the commandments of the
Lord because I feared the people and
obeyed their voice.
1 Samuel 15:24

How often are you filled with regrets? In our text, Saul has regrets because he disobeyed God. His excuse this time was that he feared the people. Do you sometimes refuse to speak or do things just to please others even though you know what you are doing or not doing is wrong? When facing temptation or difficult decisions, following the right path will allow you to have "no regret." Just do what is right!! Sounds easy, but we all know it is not possible. We all live with regrets because of actions or words we have spoken. When we do fail, we still have hope. Jesus has come to free us from the guilt of our past and lifts us up out of our despair of regret. What is God calling you to do today? When you follow Jesus, you will have "no regrets."

GOLDEN OPPORTUNITIES

The Lord rewards every man for his
righteousness and his faithfulness.
1 Samuel 26:23

Did you ever have a "golden opportunity" to get ahead, or to make a lot of money, or to win a game? David in our text had a "golden opportunity" to take the life of Saul, his enemy. David refused to act because he knew that taking Saul's life would be wrong. When you have an opportunity before you, stop and think and pray. If I take advantage of this "golden opportunity" would it be pleasing to God? Will the action you take be a righteous one? Would it reflect positively on your walk with the Lord? *Help us, Lord, to carefully evaluate the opportunities given to us that we may be righteous and faithful in what we do. Amen.*

CHAOS

There was a long war between the house of Saul and the house of David.
2 Samuel 3:1

Do you like chaos? I am sure the answer we would all give is a big no. Yet all around us we see seemingly endless chaos whether that is in politics, nations against nations, or in our own lives. In our text, the chaos is played out between factions in Israel. When we are in the midst of chaos it is hard to see what the outcome will be, but we are reminded that our God can even use chaos to bring about His plans. The Lord is with us as we ask His hand to guide us. For David it took a number of years of conflict before the chaos ended. We also wait for our deliverance. *Thank You, Lord, that even in the midst of chaos You are with us. Amen.*

FAMILY FEUD

And a messenger came to David saying:
"the hearts of the men of Israel have
gone after Absalom."
2 Samuel 15:13

There is a TV game show called: "Family Feud." A game show is a big difference from a real "family feud." Sadly, in life, there are too many families where there is no communication between loved ones. In David's case, his son is rebelling. David, for his part, had refused to meet with his son for over four years. Are you facing a difficult situation now in your family? Know that the Lord is with you during this trial. Is there something that the Lord might want you to say or do? David waited too long, and then it was too late to do anything. How wonderful to know our Heavenly Father is always there for us, His arms are opened, and in fact He reaches out to us with His love and forgiveness. There are no "family feuds" with our heavenly Father that Jesus cannot heal.

SLEEP

I lay down and slept; I wake again,
for the Lord sustained me.
Psalm 3:5

There is something that we all have in common, and that is the necessity of sleep. Every night, around the world, people will fall asleep. Some nights sleep is better than others! Falling asleep is good but waking up is amazing! During our time of sleep, the world keeps going, our hearts keep beating, and we are aware of nothing. Then we awake, ready to go. Sleep is something we all do and can easily take for granted. Each time we awake is a great opportunity for us to join with David, the writer of this psalm and saying: *Thank You, Lord, for the night. Thank You for sustaining me throughout my time of sleeping, and for granting me this new day. Amen.*

BAD ADVICE

Is it because there is no God in Israel that you
are going to inquire of the god of Ekron?
2 Kings 1:2

When you are facing decisions in life, who do you turn to for wise advice? In our text, the king wanted to hear from an idol. What? "Bad advice!" This seems beyond foolish for a king to do, but yet, how often do we turn to the wrong sources for advice? Do the opinions of others seem more important to you than the counsel of God's Word. Good advice can be found! We know that God's Word guides us. We can turn to the Lord in prayer. We can ask godly men or women as well. Disaster can follow with "bad advice." *Dear Lord, thank You for Your Word, and help me to follow godly advice in my decisions. Amen.*

PEOPLE

Jehosheba took Joash and stole him away from among the king's sons who were being put to death, and she put him and his nurse in a bedroom.
2 Kings 11:2

Are you an ordinary person? Did you know that the Lord uses ordinary people to do extraordinary work in His kingdom? In our text, a woman and a nurse would hide the future king in a bedroom for seven years. "Ordinary people," made an enormous difference in saving a life. As you look back on your life, think about the "ordinary people" that God has used to bless you. Especially those who have helped you grow in your walk with Jesus. Perhaps it is a VBS teacher, or a friend, or a family member. Then look for ways you can be used by the Holy Spirit to be a blessing to someone else. With the help of God, "ordinary people" can do amazing work in sharing the love of Jesus. *Dear Lord, thank You for the ordinary people who have touched my life with Your love. Amen.*

TRUST ME!

It is better to take refuge in the
Lord than to trust in man.
Psalm 118:8

Recently I turned on the TV with a goal in mind to get the weather report. To my dismay, before I could find out the weather, I heard a number of political ads. If one would summarize the ads, the main premise appears to be: "trust me, and do not trust my opponent." Our text reminds us of the one we can trust with no doubt in our minds. When you are faced with a dilemma remember these words: "It is better to take refuge in the Lord." Knowing we can trust the Lord whatever situation we find ourselves gives us the peace that we need. By the way, I did finally hear the weather: "This is the day the Lord has made, let us be glad and rejoice in it." *(Psalm 118:24)* That is a weather report you can trust!

JOYFULNESS

Make a joyful noise to the Lord all the earth
Serve the Lord with gladness!
Come into his presence with singing!
Psalm 100:1

Did you know there is another contagious bug running around? This bug has no known cure. The bug is "joyfulness." One of the places where this infection is found is in worship. As we are reminded of the saving grace of Jesus, as we hear the Word proclaimed, and receive absolution, the "joyfulness" bug finds willing hosts in our hearts and minds. When Pastor Schultz was installed, you could see the "joyfulness" bug as well. Whenever you feel down and out, and we all do at times, get exposed to the "joyfulness" bug as you come to worship. *Thank You, Lord, for giving us the bug of "joyfulness" as we are reminded of Your amazing grace. Amen.*

POLITICAL ADS

I urge that supplications, prayers…be made for all people…and for all who are in high positions.
2 Timothy 2:2

'Tis the season of political ads played over and over on radio and TV. How do you respond to the message? If you are like me, you probably just roll your eyes. In our text, another response is encouraged. Pray! When the name is mentioned, whether the person is in office or seeking office, pray for that person. Pray that their decisions would be wise and godly. Pray for them and their families. And pray that we, as Jesus followers, might choose the right leaders. When we pray for all people, we are united even if our votes are different. Instead of rolling our eyes, we can lift our eyes to heaven in prayer and use the ad time as prayer time. *Thank You, Lord, for those who serve our country, protect them and may they be guided by Your Word. Amen.*

COURAGE

His heart was courageous in the ways of the Lord.
2 Chronicles 17:6

How do you measure courage? We know individuals who courageously fight cancer, or we hear of a soldier on the battlefield who is courageous. Our missionaries are courageous as they serve in difficult circumstances. Today we hear of Jehoshaphat. Although I know of no one with that name today, he is someone who modeled true "courage." How? He was zealous in following God's commands, and in sharing God's Word with the people in his kingdom. Today it takes "courage" to follow the Lord. We need to ask ourselves this question: "Am I courageous in the ways of the Lord?" All of us have failed, but it takes "courage" to move forward with the help of God. *Thank You, Lord, for courageous men and women. Help me to be courageous in following Your Word. Amen.*

ENDURANCE

Let us run with endurance the race that
is set before us, looking to Jesus.
Hebrews 12: 1-2

Long distance running is a sport that takes "endurance." My grandson is a long-distance runner. He does not take after his grandfather! In our Christian walk, it is important to finish strong in the faith all the way to the end of our lives. That is not an easy task. Last week I mentioned Jehoshaphat; he started strong then stumbled as he grew older. How do we keep going? I am not sure what a runner does, but as a follower of Jesus we do not look inwardly for strength, but outwardly. We look to Jesus. He provides the "endurance" we need with His forgiveness as the Holy Spirit gives us the guidance we need along the way. Starting strong in the faith is important, but it takes "endurance" to finish the race set before us. If you are tired of running your race, remember to turn to Jesus for the strength and support that you need.

HELP NEEDED

I know that through your prayers and
the help of the Spirit of Jesus Christ, this
will turn out for my deliverance.
Philippians 1:19

Have you ever needed help? After hurricane Ian, many needed help. Some were stranded in their cars, and others were on roof tops. When you need help, you realize that there is nothing you can do to get out of a situation. Paul found that in our text, he was in prison. There was no way out. He then points out ways to get help in impossible situations. Number one is prayer. Prayer of others is a real help to those in need! Second is the help of the Holy Spirit. Paul did not know what the outcome would be. But he knew it would turn out because he was getting the "help needed." Do not forget to pray, for it is amazing to realize that our prayers can be the "help needed" for others.

THINGS HAPPEN

I want you to know that what has happened to me has really served to advance the Gospel.
Philippians 1:11

Have you ever wondered why something happened in your life? Usually, we wonder why something bad happens like a fire, or flood, or health issue. Did you ever wonder why something good happens as well? For Paul, he was in prison which sounds bad, but Paul realized this situation was really good. Why? He could share the gospel. What a great lesson for us to remember. When "things happen" look for ways that with the help of God may turn out for the good. Maybe you are being given the opportunity to share the Gospel, or to help someone in need in Jesus' name. Often, we do not know why things happen, but we can know for sure that Jesus is with us in all the happenings of our lives.

INVESTMENTS

For me to live is Christ and to die is gain.
Philippians 1:21

How are your investments doing? The answer most financial institutions will give you is something like this: "For illustrative purpose only, there is no guaranteed return." Our text steers us in another direction, toward heavenly investments. In our text, Paul encourages us to put our hope and purpose of life in Jesus. As we do that, by faith, we know that the result is eternity in heaven. What a great return, that is guaranteed not by any earthly institution, but by Jesus, Himself. If you want a great return, guaranteed, go all in with Jesus.

GIFT

By grace you have been saved through faith.
And this is not your own doing it is the gift of God.
Ephesians 2:8

Reformation is a wonderful opportunity for us to focus on the greatest gift you and I will ever receive. In the stores, Christmas is front and center as we are encouraged to buy gifts. In our communities the focus is on Halloween costumes as children seek the gift of candy as they wear creative costumes. In the church, no costume is necessary we come as we are before God. Here we hear the Good News proclaimed: "By grace you are saved through faith." We do not focus on the gifts we may receive or the number of pieces of candy a child's bag may be filled with, but instead we rest secure in the "gift" that God has already given to us. What a gift!

HEAVENLY BODIES

We await a Savior, the Lord Jesus Christ,
who will transform our lowly body
to be like his glorious body.
Philippians 4:1

When celebrating All Saints Day, we especially rejoice with those who, in the past years by faith, have entered their heavenly home. We can celebrate, and rejoice for them, even as we miss their presence with us. I am often asked: "What will we look like in heaven?" The key is in our text: "like his (Jesus) glorious body." If you want to get an idea of what Jesus looks like, read the accounts of Jesus' appearance after His resurrection, and *Revelation Chapter 1*. The good news is our "heavenly bodies" will be wonderful, stupendous, and beyond anything we can now comprehend. These bodies will not fall apart or decay and will be ours for eternity in heaven. For the believer, the best is yet to come as we remember heaven is our home.

SOLDIERS

Share in suffering as a good soldier of Christ Jesus.
2 Timothy 2:3

November 11each year is set aside in our country as Veterans Day. In my office is a triangular box with an American flag in it which reminds me of my dad who was a veteran. We pray for and are grateful for those who serve or have served in the six branches of the armed forces. We are reminded in our text that all believers are soldiers in the army of God. We became a soldier through our baptism. Welcome to the army of the Lord! Serving as a soldier involves suffering. When we hear the accounts of veterans we are humbled at their sacrifice. May we follow their example as we serve as soldiers of the cross today. We pray: *Lord of the Armies, please protect us and all the soldiers of our country wherever they serve. Amen.*

APPRECIATION

I thank my God every time I remember you.
Philippians 1:3

How do you show appreciation? One easy way is to say the words: Thank You! This is very important in relationships. Too often you hear the complaint of a spouse saying: "He (or she) does not appreciate me." How do they know? Part of the problem is that they do not say thank you to one another. Today I would like to say "thank you" to the members of St. Paul. If you are reading this that means you! For your kindness to me, for your cards of thanks, and for your warm greetings when I see you. Most of all I thank God that you are partners in sharing the Good News of Jesus. Together as a congregation, through the power of the Holy Spirit, the message of hope is shared. I appreciate you!

GIVE THANKS TO GOD

Always giving thanks to God the Father for everything in the name of our Lord Jesus Christ.
Ephesians 5:19

Often when friends are gathered around the Thanksgiving table, the question is asked, "What are you thankful for?" One child shouted: "I am thankful for everything except the beans." We are to be thankful always and for everything. We give thanks to our heavenly Father for He is good! We give thanks for our blessings in the name of our Lord Jesus Christ. Through Jesus we see the abundant love God has for us. Martin Luther states it well in his explanation of the First Article of the Apostles' Creed: "All this He does only out of fatherly, divine goodness and mercy, without any merit or worthiness in me. For all this it is my duty to thank and praise, serve and obey Him. This is most certainly true."

COME LORD JESUS

"Surely I am coming soon," Amen, Come, Lord Jesus!
The grace of the Lord Jesus be with all. Amen.
Revelation 22:20-21

The year is coming to a close. Outside of the weather, there probably will not be any noticeable differences between December 31 and January 1. Yet, there is a feeling of hope and promise as the New Year begins. Are you looking forward to the New Year? In our scripture reading from Revelation the author, St John, is looking forward not to a New Year, but to something much bigger. The Lord's return! We may hope for many things in the New Year, but is the return of the Lord on our list? When Christ returns, time will warp into eternity, and all will be new. We join the words of our text by saying: "Amen, Come, Lord Jesus." We do not know when, but we know Jesus will come again! Until that time, Happy New Year and may the grace of the Lord Jesus be with you all!

I WILL

The Lord Almighty has sworn, Surely, as I have planned, so it will be, and as I have purposed, so it will stand.
Isaiah 14:24

Have you ever made a commitment? I will pray more, or I will be a better son or daughter, or I will be a better mother or father. These statements are great, but you and I need to add a statement to commitments we make: "with the help of God." In our text, we are reminded that the "I will" statements that God makes do not fail. Hear those words: "so it will be...so it will stand." When you read the words of Jesus, you can have the assurance that they will not change or waver. Take a moment to read *John 3:16-17* and be blessed by this great statement of God's love!

TWO R's

Though your sins are like scarlet, they
shall be white as snow.
Isaiah 1:18

At the beginning of the New Year, we may make resolutions we hope to keep. One comic wrote: "Resolutions are your to do list for the first week of the year." In our text, we are pointed not to resolutions, but instead to repentance. We often "resolve" to do better, or stop a sinful habit, or…. These resolutions are wonderful, and should be made, but how often do we fail to keep them? Here is where the second R, repentance, is so crucial. We turn to our Savior in repentance and hear His wonderful words of forgiveness. Both R's have a place in our lives, but only in repentance followed by Jesus's forgiveness do we find the hope we need as we begin another year. *Thank You, Lord, for blessing us even in our failures with the forgiveness that You alone can give. Help me to forgive others as You have forgiven me. Amen.*

UNKINDNESS

In a surge of anger I hid my face from you
for a moment, but with everlasting kindness
I will have compassion on you.
Isaiah 54:8

How often have you been tempted to be unkind to someone? In a moment of anger when someone offends you, or ignores you, how do you react? For example, you wait in line to talk to someone and as you begin the conversation their phone rings and they answer it ignoring you! Or your friend spends their time on their cell phone instead of talking to you? When dealing with a feeling of unkindness, be reminded of our how our Lord deals with us. "Everlasting kindness" is the amazing promise in our text. We often deserve God's anger, but He chooses to give us kindness instead. *Thank You, Jesus, for Your love and kindness, toward us! Help me to show that same undeserved kindness toward others. Amen.*

QUARRELING

Woe to him who quarrels with his Maker.
Isaiah 45:9

In most families, there is a fair degree of quarreling. This can be especially true amongst siblings who will quarrel over important things like: "whose turn is it to be first?" Our text warns us against quarrelling with God, and later in the verse states it this way: "does the clay say to the potter, 'what are you making?' Knowing God has made me, died for me, and that I am in His hands, can give us confidence that even the difficult circumstances of life will be shaped according to His will. We may not know what the outcome may be, but we are surrounded by His loving hands!

COME OUT, COME OUT WHEREVER YOU ARE!

Saying to the prisoners, "Come out,"
to those who are in darkness, "Appear."
Isaiah 49:9

Playing hide and seek is great fun with children. The goal is to hide, so no one can find you. If you are successful, the seeker will finally shout: "Come out come out wherever you are!" The Lord calls to us as well. When we sin, our first response may be to hide. Remember Adam and Eve? We do not want to face the Lord and others. The Lord calls to those who are prisoners in their sin to come. Stop hiding and confess your sin. Then you will not receive judgement, but rather forgiveness. Remember, Jesus died to set prisoners free. *Thank You, Jesus, for forgiving our sin, help us to come out of hiding to serve You and others. Amen.*

WHAT BUSINESS ARE YOU IN?

Then Jesus came from Galilee to the Jordon to John to be baptized by him.
Matthew 3:13

This verse is signaling a change in the way of life for Jesus. Life would never be the same for Him after His baptism. Jesus knew what His job was. Jesus would heal, teach, and train His disciples, but His job would be to suffer and die for us. As we see His mission and purpose for His life, we as children of God through our baptism have a similar calling. We are to do our heavenly Father's business. Too often we find ourselves wanting to do our own thing, rather than what the Lord has called us to do. Lent is a good time to reflect and to remind ourselves that our calling is to follow God's will for our lives. Lent is a time to stop, and to reflect, and to seek the Lord and His direction for our lives. The words of a hymn come to mind as our prayer: "Oh that the Lord would guide my ways. To keep His statutes still! Oh, that my God would grant me grace, to know and do His will!"

THE ONLY CURE

God demonstrated his own love for us in this:
While we were still sinners, Christ died for us.
Romans 5:8

When you have a serious medical condition, you will want to be with a specialist who knows what they are doing. You do not want someone to look at you and say: "wow, I have never seen this before!" Spiritually we are in a much more serious condition, we have a recurring condition that needs the healing that only one specialist can give. Our spiritual diagnosis: sinner. Our specialist: Jesus. We are blessed with knowing that Jesus knows our condition all too well, and He offers the only cure. A doctor may prescribe some medicine and say that this should help you. Our spiritual doctor says, this is the cure, I died for you! My blood was shed, that you might be forgiven. What great news that is for us!

SPRING BREAK

Then Jesus went back across the Jordan to the place where John had been baptizing in the early days.
John 10:40

Some of us look to get away for a spring break somewhere warm. We want to get away for a while! Jesus is doing something similar. He is getting away from Jerusalem and those who were wanting to seize Him. He went back to a place of good memories of His baptism by John at the Jordan. When we are stressed, going back to a happier time is helpful. I like to go back at times to see places I lived before to recall some good memories. Jesus is teaching us that it is okay to get away for a time of prayer and reflection. Jesus would soon return to Jerusalem, but He would be ready to face those who would seize Him. When facing a difficult time, try following example of Jesus so that you might be encouraged and renewed in your walk with the Lord. I am reminded of these words of promise from God's Word: "He leads me beside quiet waters, he restores my soul." *(Psalm 23:2)*

RANSOM
O Come, O Come, Emmanuel

O come, O come Emmanuel,
And ransom captive Israel,
That mourns in lonely exile here
Until the Son of God appears.

A group of men, women, and children on a mission trip to Haiti were kidnapped by a gang which is demanding a ransom for their release. As I write this, we are still praying for their release. Just as these captives need help, all of us need the help that only the coming of "Emmanuel" can bring. We cannot make it on our own. We too need ransom because of our sinful disobedience. The birth of Jesus who is "Emmanuel," brings us a secure rescue. He comes to ransom us by the sacrifice of His life. As you look at the birth of Jesus, rejoice because the "Son of God" appears! The great news of Christmas is in knowing we are no longer captives; we have been set free! For as we gaze at the cradle, we also see the cross and empty tomb. "Everyone who calls on the name of the Lord will be saved." *(Romans 10:13)*

WISDOM
O Come, O Come, Emmanuel

O Come Thou Wisdom from on high,
Who ord'rest all things mightily
To us the path of knowledge show,
And teach us in her ways to go.

Would you say the world is a mess? Despite all our so-called "wisdom" and knowledge, there is a lot of strife and confusion. The smartest countries of the world fight each other, and poorer countries suffer under the burden of corruption and poverty. Political correctness often flies in the face of Scriptural correctness. In the midst of this Christmas comes the wisdom of a baby in the manger. As you hear verse two of our hymn, remember the message of Jesus. His message is real wisdom for those who believe but foolishness for those who do not. The words of Paul come to mind, "For God has chosen the foolish things of the world to shame the wise, and God has chosen the weak things of the world to shame the things which are strong." *(1 Corinthians 1:2)* True wisdom is found in Jesus who was crucified for you.

AWE
O Come, O Come, Emmanuel

O come, O come, thou Lord of might,
Who to Thy tribes on Sinai's height
In ancient times didst give the Law
In cloud and majesty and awe.

What gives you "awe?" I can guarantee that if you were standing near Mount Sinai when God thundered from the mountain, you would have been in awe! This awe was followed by Moses coming down the mountain and giving the tablets of the law. On Christmas night, the awe was different. This time it was the shepherds out in the field who were awed by the host angels that appeared to them. In this case, the announcement was the birth of a Savior who is Christ the Lord. Amazingly, as God opened the gates of heaven that night, the focus was a baby. The babe was "Emmanuel" which means "God with us." He came to fulfill the law in order to bring forgiveness and salvation to all who believe. May we be awed this day as we remember our God, our Savior, the Lord of might.

\

WICKEDNESS

Attend to me, and answer me;
I moan because of the oppression of the wicked.
Psalm 55:2-5

Tragically, we hear the horrific accounts of wickedness in our world. In reading *Psalm 55*, David describes this wickedness in vivid terms, and even recounts how those who once were friends turned against him. Wickedness is not new. In the midst of our anger and our sorrow over wickedness, there is a beautiful six-word conclusion to this Psalm. May these simple, yet powerful words be our prayer as we face the wickedness of life: "But I will trust in You." *Dear Lord, as we face moments of tragedy and sorrow in our lives and in our nation, help us to remember that our hope and peace is found by trusting in You.*

WHY SHOULD CROSS AND TRIAL GRIEVE ME

1 Why should cross and trial grieve me?
Christ is near With His cheer; Never will He leave me.
Who can rob me of the heaven That
God's Son For me won
When His life was given?

Looking at the words of the first verse of this hymn, I am struck at how well the author, Paul Gerhardt, hits the truth of the matter regarding trials. He first admits it is a trial...but then with the help of God he says should I let trial grieve me? The answer: Christ is near with His cheer. I like to see that cheer as being our Savior saying He is with us. Those words "He will never leave me" are always an awesome thought for us. I never use the word never about myself. IE: I will never do that again. Because as soon as I say that, bingo, I do it again. Jesus is the only one that can truly say, I will never leave you. When we are robbed of our health, or strength to play golf, that is a lousy situation. Then we are reminded that "nothing can rob me of heaven." So, we say, Yeah God. His Son gave His life for me.

WHY SHOULD CROSS AND TRIAL GRIEVE ME

2 When life's troubles rise to meet me,
Though their weight May be great,
They will not defeat me.
God, my loving Savior, sends them; He who knows
All my woes Knows how best to end them.

As a friend had his last chemo, I shared verse 1 of this hymn with him. Verse 2 is also full of dynamic thoughts. Receiving chemo cannot be easy. And from what I heard, the days following are the toughest part. Obviously, you know this better than I do. The weight of troubles is great as the song states so clearly. Then comes the clear words: they WILL NOT defeat me. That is the determination I know that you have. We know this is only possible with the help of God of course. The words "God, my loving Savior sends them," is tough for me to fully comprehend. However, I remember our discussions in the past, as we prayed for others going through trials, that we knew that all of us will have trials. When they come, our response is not why me but why not me. The comfort is in the words "my loving Savior." Knowing He is there making all the difference. As we pray for healing and strength, we have confidence in knowing as the last verse states so beautifully the Lord is there, and our troubles will one day end. And His plan is best.

BEHOLD THE LAMB OF GOD

Behold the Lamb of God who takes
away the sin of the world.
John 1:29

The opening line of a favorite hymn of the church is this, "Just as I am without one plea." Perhaps you have many verses of this hymn memorized. How sobering to reflect on those frightening words. Today we are hearing pleas for help from the people of Ukraine. These are desperate cries. "Please help us" as much of the world is in mourning because of their plight. As individuals, we plea for help for there is no relief from the guilt of our sinful condition. In the midst of our desperation, we hear the words of our text: "Behold the Lamb of God." The impossible has become possible because of Jesus' blood shed for me and you. *Thank You, Lord, for saving us for without You we would have no hope. Help all those who plead to You this day. Amen.*

DARK BLOT
Just as I Am, without One Plea

2 Just as I am and waiting not
To rid my soul of one dark blot,
To Thee, whose blood can cleanse each spot,
O Lamb of God, I come, I come.

By His wounds you have been healed.
1 Peter 2:24

The second verse of the hymn "Just as I am" has these haunting words: "Just as I am and waiting not To rid my soul of one dark blot." Do you have a dark blot in your life? The blot could be a sin you committed and now deeply regret, or the blot could be an offense against you. The great news we can proclaim is that we do not have to wait any longer for the removal of that dark blot. The blood of Christ has cleansed you from that one dark blot. Like a stain on a garment that is removed and is no longer there after a wash, so too the "dark blot" of sin is removed. When that memory comes up again in your mind, know that you can give thanks to Jesus for the removal of the blots in your life. Ask Jesus to help you to turn your feelings of guilt or hurt to rejoicing in His forgiveness and love.

TOSSED ABOUT

Just as I Am, without One Plea

3 Just as I am, though tossed about
With many a conflict many a doubt,
Fightings and fears within without
O Lamb of God, I come, I come.

And whoever comes to me I will never cast out.
John 6:37

Tossing about at night is an experience many have had at one time or another. We go over and over in our minds something that has happened to us or something that we have done, or a fear of tomorrow. As we are tossing about, we may try and convince ourselves to be at rest. The comforting words of our text and hymn verse remind us that no matter what condition we are in, or no matter what we are feeling inside, we can have a rock-solid promise from our Savior, "I will never cast you out." As a child of God, we can come to Jesus in the midst of our "tossing about" and know He has His arms around us. *Thank You, Jesus, that You are with me during those times I find myself tossed about. Amen.*

JUST AS I AM
Just as I Am, without One Plea

4 Just as I am, poor wretched, blind;
Sight, riches, healing of the mind,
Yeah, all I need, in Thee I find,
O Lamb of God, I come, I come.

When hearing the words "poor, wretched, blind" our first thought might be about someone who is facing physical hardships. The song is really pointing to the spiritual blindness we often have. This blindness makes it difficult to see our sin as well as to see the awesomeness of God's grace. As a result, our minds can be troubled. We recognize how messed up and confused we can often be. The assurance that we have is no matter what our condition there is One we can turn to "Just as I am," and that is Jesus. He is here to provide the healing that we need. *Thank You, Lord, for Your grace, and healing in our lives. Amen.*

JUST AS I AM

Just as I Am, without One Plea

5 Just as I am, Thou wilt receive
Wilt welcome, pardon, cleanse, relieve.
Because Thy promise I believe,
O Lamb of God, I come, I come.

There are many who suffer because of emotional or mental pain. Those who face these issues often try to go on with life and pretend nothing is wrong. Sadly, too many turn to solutions such as drugs or even suicide to help relieve their pain. Fortunately, we do not have to hide our pain from Jesus. We can come to Him no matter what our condition, and know He is there for us. No matter what you are facing cling to the promises of God who brings: "pardon, cleansing, and relief." *Lord, be with us and those who struggle this day. As we turn to You, strengthen our trust in Your promises. Amen.*

BROKEN BARRIER
Just as I Am, without One Plea

6 Just as I am; Thy love unknown
Has broken ev'ry barrier down,
Now to be Thine, yea, Thine alone,
O Lamb of God, I come, I come

We all face barriers in life. The one barrier we have in common is death. When facing death, we are looking at a barrier we only experience once. One person said to me when asked if he feared dying simply said, "I have never done this before." When facing death, we look at the amazing love of Jesus. Jesus, the one who died and rose again from the grave has "broken the barrier" of death. When you and I face that final barrier, we can simply say, "O Lamb of God, I come." Then enfolded in the arms of Jesus, we will experience anew His amazing love. Jesus said as recorded in *John 14:3*, "I go and prepare a place for you, I will come again and will take you to myself, that where I am you may be also." Jesus has broken ev'ry barrier down!

FOCUS

I Know That My Redeemer Lives

2 He lives triumphant from the grave;
He lives eternally to save;
He lives all glorious in the sky;
He lives exalted there on high.

Each morning when you wake up, what is the first thing that you do? Each of us have our morning routines, but for those of us who wear glasses or contacts, fairly soon in the morning we put our spectacles on so we can see. Before we do, everything is out of focus, but once they are on things look clearer again. On Easter, we were able to focus on those words, "He Lives." Yes, our surroundings were different, but the glorious resurrection account is unchanging. Whenever things seem out of focus in our lives, it is good to remember those words of this song, "He lives triumphant, eternally, all glorious, and exalted!" *Help us, Lord, at all times to keep our focus on You and the great news of the resurrection. Amen.*

COMPLAINT
I Know That My Redeemer Lives

4 He lives to grant me rich supply;
He lives to guide me with His eye;
He lives to comfort me when faint;
He lives to hear my soul's complaint.

Here is a thought: how about declaring a day in April as, "A Day of Complaining!" Let us be honest, we have plenty to complain about. In Wisconsin, the weather in April is usually a good source of complaint, or the shortage of our favorite foods, or being stuck in the house with the same people all the time, or not being able to golf, etc. We usually will say words like, "Stop Complaining" or "It could be worse." However, on this "Day of Complaining" there are to be no excuses as to why we do not complain. This stanza of the hymn is interesting, "He lives to hear my soul's complaint." Jesus is not blown away by our complaining and He loves us just the same. Complaining is a natural part of our lives then as we focus again on our Lord, we find the solace that we seek in His grace. *Thank You, Lord, that You hear our complaints and love us just the same. Amen.*

THE IF'S OF LENT
An IF And a But

And one of the malefactors railed on Him, saying: If You be Christ, save Thyself and us BUT the other rebuked him.
Luke 23:39 KJV

The scene on Good Friday was horrific. Jesus is on the cross, and even as He is suffering and dying the taunting continues. The dying thief is not the only one who taunts Him. The soldier's state: "If Thou be the king of the Jews save Thyself," the rulers say the same words as do others going by. Mocking Jesus to the end, there is one bright light, one thief turns to Jesus for life.

THE IF'S OF LENT
The Threatening IF

If you release this man you are not
a friend of Caesar's.
John 19:12

Threatening IFs are common. If you don't do this, then you are not a part of the group. If you are known as a Christian, you can be labeled as a Jesus freak. Or, we have seen many told, "If you are a Christian, then you will be killed." Pilate was being threatened with being labeled as no friend of Caesar–a very serious charge at the time. This decision by Pilate would label him for all eternity as the one who crucified Jesus. As you face those "Threatening If's" in your life, ask the Lord for the strength to make the right stand for your faith. Pilate failed to listen, even to his wife. May you, with the help of God, stand ready to do what is right no matter what the consequences may appear to be.

THE IF'S OF LENT
The Proving IF

By this all people will know that you are my disciples, if you have love of one another.
John 13:35

How does the world identify a follower of Christ? Many people will wear a cross. Does that mark you as a follower of Christ? As I have observed those who wear crosses, I wonder sometimes if they are a follower of Christ. A car was pulled over, and the driver was asked for proof of ownership. The officer then said, "I thought this car was stolen. I saw the bumper sticker saying, 'Jesus saves' and observed the way you were driving and thought for sure the car was stolen." Ouch! Do you show love for others even behind the wheel? Jesus showed His disciples what love is all about. During Lent, we see His willingness to suffer and die because He loved us. Our call, to love one another and showing that love to others, they will know what the cross you are wearing means! *Father, thank You for Your love for us, forgive us when we fail to love as we should. Help us to follow Jesus' example of love in all that we do. Amen.*

THE IF'S OF LENT
The IF of Submission

Jesus prayed: "My Father, if this cup cannot be taken away unless I drink it; let your will be done."
Matthew 26:42

"Do I have to?" That is a question that children often ask when told to do something. If we are honest, even as adults we have that same attitude. By nature, we are often rebellious. We want to do what we want to do, rather than do what others tell us to do. Jesus shows us another way: the way of submission. Here on the night before His death, we see that Jesus was willing to do what His heavenly Father told Him to do. Submission can be costly! Yet, we are called to follow the example of Jesus by submitting to the commands of God. *Lord, forgive me of my rebellion against Your Word, help me to follow Jesus' example when He submitted to Your commands. Amen.*

THE IF'S OF LENT
The Two IF's

"If you are the Christ, tell us." But he said to them,
"If I tell you, you will not believe, and if I ask you,
you will not answer."
Luke 22:67-68

This text reveals the malice of those who were putting Jesus on trial. In a mocking tone they shout, "IF you are the Christ." Their hearts were already hardened, and Jesus by His two if's responses, stated that He knew what was in their hearts. Have you ever treated someone the way Jesus was treated? The person may ask you to forgive them, and you say no. Or perhaps you are just too stubborn to listen to wise counsel. "I have made up my mind and nothing you can say will change it." Our stubbornness or pride can lead us to sin. Fortunately, Jesus sees through to our heart. He loved us and died so that we might be forgiven even of the malice or stubbornness of our hearts. *Thank you, Lord, for loving us and forgiving us, please help us to listen to You as we should. Amen.*

THE IF'S OF LENT
The Comparative IF

If they do these things when the wood is green, what will happen when it is dry?
Luke 23:31

These words of Jesus were spoken as He carried His cross and serve as a warning to us of the deadly nature of sin. Imagine you hire someone to trim your bushes in the spring, but instead of cutting off the dead branches, the live green ones are cut and only the dead ones remain. Jesus is like that green branch which is cut down on the cross to pay for our sins. We are like the dead branches because of sin. What would you do with a bush with only dead branches? The answer is obvious. This IF of Lent reminds us that the wage of sin is death! We dare not take our sins lightly. During this coming Holy Week of Lent, we thank Jesus for His willingness to suffer and die for us.

THE IF'S OF LENT
The Evasive IF

So Pilate came out to them and asked: "What accusations are you making against this man?" The Jews answered: "If he weren't a criminal we wouldn't have handed him over to you."
John 18:29-30

The Jews were caught in their own scheme. Their original false accusation of blasphemy had to be changed to something else because that was not a punishable crime. They were evasive and misleading. Their IF in reality was their own guilty sentence. Have you ever falsely accused someone, or have you ever been falsely accused? We can so easily let our mouths run riot either deliberately or as a so-called innocent repeater of a rumor, or insinuation, or by drawing a conclusion. Thankfully, Jesus died to forgive us for making false accusations, and we with the help of God can forgive others who have falsely accused us. The "Evasive IF" is a great reminder to us as we see how a false accusation led to Jesus' crucifixion. *Forgive us, Lord, for the times we have falsely accused others, and help us to forgive as we have been forgiven. Amen.*

THE IF'S OF LENT
The IF of Easter

If Christ had not been raised, then our preaching
is in vain and your faith is in vain.
1 Corinthians 15:14

There is no statement more powerful than the triumphant words on Easter morning, "He is Risen!" The resurrection of Jesus from the dead changes everything. The heart and soul of our faith is knowing that because Jesus lives, we shall live also. Without that knowledge, our faith would be simply an interesting philosophy. I have ministered at the bedside of those who were 40 minutes old and those who were 101 years old. In each case the dynamic words are the same, "I go to prepare a place for You" and "He that believes and is baptized shall be saved!" There is no IF about the resurrection. When you are facing life or death, remember the Resurrection of Jesus Christ from the dead. He is Risen! He is Risen, indeed!

Made in the USA
Coppell, TX
30 August 2023